The 7 Secrets of Ef

The 7 SECRETS *of* Effective Fathers

Ken R. Canfield

TYNDALE HOUSE PUBLISHERS, INC.
Wheaton, Illinois

Library of Congress Cataloging-in-Publication Data

Canfield, Ken R.
  The seven secrets of effective fathers / Ken R. Canfield.
      p.   cm.
  Includes bibliographical references.
  ISBN 0-8423-5915-X
    1. Fathers—United States.   2. Father and child—United States.
3. Fathers—Religious life.   I. Title.   II. Title: 7 secrets of
effective fathers.
HQ756.C358   1992
306.874′2—dc20   92-17686

Printed in the United States of America

98 97 96 95 94 93 92
9   8   7   6   5   4   3   2   1

To him who is calling out fathers throughout the land

Acknowledgments

This book has been produced with the skills and insights of many people. Yet there are certain indispensable persons who have helped in the birth process. I gratefully acknowledge their contributions. First, my wife, Dee. She has insight and discernment far beyond her years. She has constantly encouraged me that the vision for equipping fathers is right for our time. Second, Lowell Bliss and the staff of the National Center for Fathering. Lowell is one of the key players who has helped to shape much of our scientific material into good readable stuff. Brock Griffin has made a valuable contribution in editing and setting the tone of the writing.

Judd Swihart, Suzan Hawkes, Ken Kennedy, and Gary Klozenbucher have given consistent encouragement and feedback over the years. Organizationally Chuck Aycock, Blake Ashdown, and Emerson Eggerichs have helped to insure that the research and direction of the National Center for Fathering is more than a flash in the pan.

Finally, Tyndale House Publishers, through the vision of Ron Beers and the superb editing of Ken Petersen, have gone the extra mile to make this an important book. I concur with the words of Pascal as I reflect on the research and writing contained herein: "Certain authors, speaking of their works, say, 'My book,' 'My commentary,' 'My history,' etc. . . . They would do better to say, 'Our book,' 'Our commentary,' 'Our history,' etc., because there is in them usually more of other people's than their own."

Contents

Contents

One

The Voices
of Effective
Fathers

It's 2:45 A.M. and I'm in my office, sitting in front of a computer screen, its bluish glow the only light in the room. My eyes are beginning to blur, so I rub them, then refocus. I am physically tired, but my mind is alive, stimulated by the phosphor numbers in front of my eyes. What I see is absolutely fascinating.

Four thousand voices from fathers across America. That's how many men have been surveyed by the National Center for Fathering. Their responses, answers, comments, and experiences are painting statistical pictures on my computer monitor.

For the past five years I've spent countless hours running statistical tests, reading diverse scientific journals, and interacting with other professionals who are working with fathers. And, yes, I've also been raising five children of my own. I have often thought, *Fathering can't be all that complex; men have been doing it for centuries, haven't they?* But as soon as I ask that question, my mind conjures up pictures of my children at home in their beds. I see my daughter Hannah, who will be a teenager before long, and I know that as she matures and begins to stretch her wings, I'm going to be facing some of my toughest times as

3

a dad. I think of the others—Sarah, Joel, and Micah. I picture Rachel, breathing steadily in her crib.

Yes, fathering *is* a daunting and complex task. My children and your children are unique human beings created in the image of God. They are growing up to have their own lives, something we as parents can never control completely. Our fathering is further complicated by this world in which we live, with its increasing expectations, tight economics, and competing pressures. Our fathering is even more complicated by our relationships with our own fathers, many of whom were physically absent or emotionally distant.

I once asked a group of men at a fathering seminar to write a one-sentence word picture describing how they felt about their fathering. One man wrote, "I feel like a dachshund dog running in deep snow."

Can you identify? I can.

It sends me back to the research with an even greater urgency. You see, among all the fathers that the National Center has surveyed have been a number of men who are considered by professionals, peers, and their churches to be particularly *effective* fathers. These men are not child psychologists or clergymen. They are dads just like you and me, but they have taken their fathering role strongly to heart and have excelled in it. They are master craftsmen. I listen to these men because I want their wisdom and insights on how I, too, can become an effective father.

We've studied these men. In particular, we've looked for areas of fathering practice where these effective dads scored significantly differently than all the other dads in our data bank. What do they know that the rest of us should know? What things have they done that we can accomplish in our lives?

The National Center for Fathering has found out.

There *are* certain things that effective fathers do differently than all other dads. In fact, there are at least seven things. We call them the seven secrets of effective fathers, and if we learn them, we, too, can become better fathers.

The Frustrations of Good Fathers

Even though there is a very real and distressing plague of fatherlessness in our country (see Appendix B), most men I come in contact with through the National Center are capable and well meaning. They work diligently at spending time with their kids, expressing their love, and imparting wise discipline. They have a real desire to win with their children, and they consider their kids to be an important part of their lives.

But many of them are like my friend Eric. "Ken," he told me, as we sat on the front porch and watched our kids playing across the street in the park, "I have *no* idea what I'm doing when it comes to this fathering stuff. I feel like a fish out of water."

His confession surprised me a little because he seemed very involved in his children's lives. "Oh, I feel like I'm doing everything that's expected of me most of the time," he said. "But even that's only by the grace of God, what with my job and everything. Usually, I feel like I'm just muddling through. I've got this fear that one day it's all going to crash down around me."

I've had other men tell me about being in the birthing room at the hospital, the time they held their first newborn child in their arms. The baby breathes and color rushes to her cheeks, while the father gazes in joy. But then on the way home after the delivery, a thought flashes through the new father's mind. It resurfaces again many times during those first few weeks. *Wait a second,* he thinks. *I've never been trained for this. I've gone through college or vo-tech to become a career man. I had premarital counseling to learn about being a husband. I even went to all of the LaMaze classes, but no one has ever shown me how to be a father to this child.*

Effective fathers are different. Oh, they experience the same fears and frustrations, and perhaps no one ever gave them special fathering instruction either. But somehow they move with a confidence often lacking in other dads. In addition, they go beyond the basic bread-and-butter issues of fathering—spending time with the kids, being physically nurturant, and exercising discipline—and reach a deeper level of relationship with

5

their children. They practice, perhaps intuitively, the seven secrets of effective fathers.

This book is for all of us "good fathers" who are trying hard but want to develop better fathering skills. We can learn from the art and craft of effective fathers around us.

Fathering Is Important

Your motivation to work through the seven secrets of effective fathers and apply them diligently to your fathering will be greatly enhanced if you accept three important truths.

_(1)_ The first truth has to do with the importance of fathering.

The Industrial Revolution exerted considerable influence on the role of the father in the family. Our dads and granddads and great grandfathers left the home for the factory, and fathering in America was relegated to the limited roles of financial provider and disciplinarian of last resort. It wasn't long before social scientists began to chime that, really, only the mother-child relationship is central to parenting; fathers are peripheral.

But fathers are not peripheral to parenting. They are crucial. _Children need their dads._ The importance of fathers is demonstrated by what occurs when fathers aren't in the home. Studies show that children who grow up in fatherless homes are more likely to drop out of high school, suffer from poverty, receive welfare, marry early, have children out of wedlock, divorce, commit delinquent acts, and engage in drug and alcohol use.[1]

In essence, fathers are neither worse nor better parents than mothers; they are simply a different type of parent—a male parent. Children need their father and their mother, both active, both functioning effectively in the home.

Your role and responsibility as a father are vitally important to your children's growth and health.

"Out of the Mouths of Babes"

"I feel that if there were a vote on who to give an award I would vote for the fathers."—*third grader*

"He is a Frito-Lay man. That is an important job. Because Frito-Lay means chips which is food. That is so important because that you could not live with out food."—*first grader*

"Without my father it would be like a ball without any air inside it. Whenever I'm feeling sad, he comes and cheers me up by telling me a silly joke or buying me a pack of baseball cards. . . . My dad is a hardworking man, but he still has time for me."—*sixth grader*

"Dad and I play baseball. Dad and I play soccer. We play tennis, too. I play karate with him, too. I sneak into his office and scare him. He says, 'Huh!' "—*first grader*

"He comforts me when I am not OK. He sacrifices his time when I want to do something special and he doesn't want to. . . . He always listens to my side of the story. He treats my mom very nicely, which makes me feel wanted."—*fourth grader*

"If you are needing help or are hurt, he will stop everything just for us . . . and at his job he always hurries home just to see us. . . . Last year people asked him to be mayor and he said, 'No, I'm going to spend more time with my kids.' That's why he is the best dad."—*third grader*

Fathering Is a Learned Skill

The second truth we must accept is that effective fathering must be learned. Fathering skills don't automatically accompany that Y chromosome your dad gave you. Hopefully, your dad also presented a good model of fathering. As you grew up, you could watch him, taking subconscious notes on how a man interacts with his wife and kids. Unfortunately, with the divorce rate doubling in the last forty years, many of us grew up without any accessible fathering models, let alone effective ones.[2]

As I was growing up, I had the opportunity to do summer

7

work for some licensed craftsmen, mostly electricians and bricklayers. I remember watching Jerry, my bricklaying boss, and the proficiency he'd developed over the years. From him I learned how to proportion the right amounts of mud, bricks, and wedges needed to complete a particular project. I watched Jerry take a brick in his hand. He seemed so agile and quick as he buttered the brick with mud and placed it into the right position. I noticed how he put everything he needed within reach, so he could get into a rhythm and have hundreds of bricks perfectly in place in what seemed like no time at all.

Or take Curt, the electrician I worked for. He would carefully roll his wire out on the floor before trying to pull it all through the conduit. Taking the time to unravel the kinks with his fingers assured him of a smooth pull through the pipe. Sometimes there were situations where he even had to pump soap into the pipe to make the pull easier. And then, after the wire was successfully through, he always double-checked the length before cutting it. "Measure twice, cut once," he would tell me.

There are many procedures these craftsmen have learned that make sense after you've seen them done. You say, "Of course, that's the best way to do it." But while they make sense, they aren't necessarily common sense. In other words, if you had been working alone, you probably wouldn't have done it that way. It would have become obvious to you only after you had gone through a long trial-and-error process yourself.

But what these journeymen represent are countless generations of experimentation, of searching for effectiveness and efficiency and *mastery*. They have wisdom and tricks of the trade handed down from journeyman to apprentice, journeyman to apprentice, journeyman to you. When you assist a journeyman, you learn his secrets of the trade.

As fathers, you and I need to become craftsmen. Maybe now we're apprentices, but we can *become* craftsmen.

In a moment of great love and affection, you conceived a human being, a child. What an incredible feat in and of itself! Here is flesh of your flesh, bone of your bone: a son or daughter.

How Do You Feel about Fathering?

The National Center for Fathering has asked various men to describe in a word picture how they feel about their fathering. Some sample replies are listed below. Put a check mark next to the word picture that you most closely identify with, or write one of your own in the space below.

☐ I feel like a farmer who is cultivating and working the ground.

☐ I feel like a warm summer breeze.

☐ I feel like rain that comes to the earth and then evaporates.

☐ I feel like the sun rising in the east.

☐ I feel like a lone lion roaring in the jungle.

☐ I feel like a duck out of water.

☐ I feel like a tall building downtown.

☐ I feel like the weather, highly unpredictable.

☐ I feel like a Dachshund dog running in deep snow.

☐ I feel like the hands of God holding the world.

☐ I feel like: _____.

A miracle. Two eyes. A nose. (Your nose!) A living, breathing human being who will grow up and think thoughts, and cry tears, and shake hands, and tell jokes, and fall in love, and battle the odds. It's incredible: you've fathered a child!

But however incredible that may be, we have to admit that any halfway-interested male graduate of puberty can father a child. A man I know who came out of the ghetto says, "Anyone can make a kid, but it takes a man to be a father." *Fathers need to be craftsmen.*

A newborn child is a wonder in and of herself. But what makes for a great deal of the wonder is the amount of potential wrapped up in that wrinkly purple skin. When the child takes her first breath of air, she lets out a wail, full and healthy. One day, that same child may sing a song where she hits a note so perfectly that all who hear her will suddenly realize that God is a God of incredible beauty and majesty.

That infant in the delivery room opens his eyes for the first time and blinks in discovery. Faint, blurry images, but he sees something: a light, a face, a table. Years later, that same child may open his eyes and suddenly see something he's never seen before. He may have insight into the way one chemical compound affects another and suddenly he knows: this is it, this is the cure for cancer.

In a newborn child, you have raw material that's beautiful in itself, but capable of so much more beauty. We need to shape that life and mold it. Anyone can hammer a nail into a board, but only a craftsman can built a cabinet, a house, or a home. Be a craftsman! Be skilled in your fathering! Produce in your family a thing of quality and usefulness and beauty.

Our society has shown us that trial and error doesn't usually work in the craft of fathering. By the time we learn how to do things the best way, our children may be grown—so now is the time to get started. In order to become skilled craftsmen, we must all begin as apprentices. We need to turn to other men and ask them, "Show me how to do this and do it well. What are your tricks of the trade? What are your secrets?"

Fathering Has Great Rewards

The third great truth is that while effective fathering is of overwhelming importance and often requires rigorous training, it also bears significant rewards.

Every father knows there are times of great pain, anguish, confusion, and inadequacy. But then there are other times, like when I walk into my children's room while they're asleep. How do you explain it? At that moment, it's not like they are doing anything to please me. They're just sleeping. They aren't being intelligent, athletic, obedient, or witty. They aren't actively giving me honor or doing anything to stroke my self-esteem. They're just lying there, their blond hair mussed across their pillows, their limbs tangled among paja-

Peace Corps Volunteers Study

Some years ago a study was conducted among Peace Corps volunteers. Researchers took a random sample of volunteers and split them into two roughly equal groups: those who completed their tour commitments and those who returned home early because of "problems of adjustment and conduct (including psychiatric terminations)."

Unlike many studies, this one was nearly unaffected by the volunteers' race or socioeconomic background. Almost all of them were college graduates from white, middle-class families. The study did not differentiate between reasons for father absence, "psychological" instead of physical absence, age at separation, or other father figures who may have stepped in. So an "absent" father was said to be one who was away from the child's residence, for whatever reason, during at least the child's tenth through fifteenth years.

The results were startling. Of the people who completed their duties, 9% came from absent-father backgrounds; but among those who came home early, 44% had absent fathers. The study was repeated, and again there was a wide gap of difference: 14% and 44%.

We're finding similar results in study after study. The evidence must not be ignored: *Your children need you.*

Peter Suedfeld, "Paternal Absence and Overseas Success of Peace Corps Volunteers," *Journal of Consulting Psychology* (1967: 31:424-25).

mas and blankets and stuffed teddy bears. How can I explain what I feel in those moments, when I sit on the corner of their beds and just stare at them?

The rewards of fathering are often these intangible moments. But just because the rewards are indescribable, that doesn't make them any less real or powerful.

As I am writing this, athletes are competing in the Winter Olympics in Albertville, France. Bonnie Blair has just won a gold medal in five-hundred-meter speed skating, and in front of the world's press she dedicated it to her father, who died two years ago.

It reminds me of a story from another Olympics held in France—the 1924 summer games in Paris. Bill Havens was selected to represent the United States that year in an event called Canadian singles. It was a canoeing event, a demonstration sport, in which the competitors sit in a high kneeling position and use a single paddle. Havens was good; in fact, everyone expected him to bring home the gold.

However, a few months before the Olympics, Havens learned that his wife was due to give birth sometime during the Games. He had a decision to make: the opportunity of a lifetime or . . . the opportunity of a lifetime. He made his decision. He stayed home. The team left for Paris without him. On August 1, 1924, his son Frank was born—four days *after* the Games.

Fast forward through all those summers when Bill Havens probably heard the results from every Olympic canoeing event and wondered if he'd made the right decision. But stop in 1952, the year the Summer Olympics were in Helsinki. Havens received a telegram from Helsinki that he surely wouldn't have traded for any amount of gold. The telegram read: "Dear Dad . . . Thanks for waiting around for me to get born in 1924. I'm coming home with the gold medal you should have won." It was signed, "Your loving son, Frank."

Frank Havens had just won the gold medal in the ten-thousand-meter Canadian singles canoeing event.[3]

Fathers may never get the opportunity to stand in the light of celebrity or athletic stardom, but every effective father will one day receive his gold medal. There's no telling what form that medal might come in. Perhaps it will be the squeeze of your daughter's hand, and slight tears will come to your eyes as you realize how wonderful it is to be loved by such a person. Maybe it will be a summer afternoon years from now, when you sit as an old man on the front porch in your rocker, not saying a word, simply looking out at your many happy grandchildren and enjoying the fact that you've done one of the most important jobs in the world and done it well.

But all these moments will fade momentarily from your memory at a more significant event: when you feel the weight of a divine hand on your shoulder and look up into the eyes of the Savior. He's smiling. And he says, "Well done, my good and faithful servant. I call many people to different tasks, but I called you to be a father and gave you these children—some of the most precious people in the world to me—and you raised them wonderfully. Thank you."

Two

Applying the Seven Secrets

We learn to father by following models.

This one statement embodies both the problem and the potential.

The *problem* is that with the high rate of divorce in our culture, there is a generation of fathers today who grew up without fathers of their own. Maybe this was your experience. Or maybe your father was emotionally distant or even abusive. In either case, your fathering model was inadequate, making it difficult for you to know how to be an effective father.

Fortunately, the *potential* of that statement is that poor models can always be replaced. If you had a bad fathering model while growing up, you can find a new one.

For the first time in decades, men are turning to other men to find encouragement and strength. You are not alone. There is a fathering movement afoot in this country. I see it every time I drive by our local Hardee's restaurant on Tuesday mornings. There are six guys in that window booth, sipping their coffee and talking. I know this group of men. I know what they're talking about, and it isn't the Kansas City Royals or prospects for pheasant season. They are listening to each other, identifying with each other, and encouraging each other to become the best dads they can be. This isn't a faction of the men's movement. No, it is part of a fathering movement, and it marches to the beat of a different drummer: the heartbeat of their own children.

Researching Effective Fathers

There are other models too—in particular, the effective fathers who speak through the research and profiles included in this book.

When my colleagues and I began our research, we first sought to identify the basic roles and responsibilities that fathers are called to perform. We surveyed the Bible, finding more than 1,190 verses pertaining to fathering, fatherhood, and fatherlessness. We read the historical literature. (The Puritans were prolific on the subject.) We read the scholarly journals. And then we talked to men.

The National Center for Fathering developed a test instrument called the Fathering Style Inventory. We received input on more than four hundred variables related to a man's fathering practice. Our pool of data from fathers all over America grew. Presently, there is no other ongoing base of fathering data in the United States as large as the one at the National Center. Currently the National Center has research and data on more than four thousand fathers. (A fuller description of our research, with reliability scales and validity studies, is included in Appendix A.)

Within this research, we conducted a substantial sampling of men who were identified as "effective fathers." These were selected by other men who worked in the helping professions and who understood the essentials of child rearing. There were two primary qualifications: each respondent had to have a child at least of adolescent age, and each had to exhibit outwardly his fathering commitment as a high priority. In other samplings, we asked peers to select those men in their local church who had reared their children successfully. We then surveyed these men and their wives and children to gain further data.[1]

In short, the effective fathers in our research were chosen by their peers, who identified them as being outstanding in their fathering skills.

The principles of fathering may be timeless (particularly as they are outlined in the Bible), but how they apply to your particular family you will learn best by listening to this collection of voices, the voices of effective fathers around the country. In this book, you'll hear stories of men just like you. And most of all, you'll hear the broad, deep voice of our fathering data base—four thousand voices, including those of effective fathers. It's a chorus of wisdom and encouragement.

Applying the Seven Secrets

What's the best way to go about applying the seven secrets of effective fathers?

Remember that we learn to father by following models. This means that as a reader you should (1) live with this book awhile, just like you would with any other father model (don't feel the need to accomplish everything in this book at once); and (2) make the seven secrets a point of discussion and accountability with your family and with other men.

You may want to read this book completely through once. Some of the individual chapters may seem particularly demanding, but there are only seven secrets, and by reading through you can easily get a general handle on each of them. Each chapter provides some practical tips on how to integrate that particular secret into your life.

You may feel the tendency to just jump in ("whole hog" as we say here in Kansas). Such enthusiasm is good, as it reflects a moment of high commitment, but you'll want to resist the temptation to try to accomplish everything at once. Trying to do everything at once is just too overwhelming. You'll end up being frustrated by everything you are trying to juggle. Besides, even if you don't burn out from trying to do everything at once, your children might!

Think about this: you have plenty of time to integrate each secret into your fathering experience. You'll be a father for the rest of your life. Granted, your kids may only be under your roof for a while, but even then, you'll have decades with the youngest, and hours and months and years with the oldest. *Don't ever underestimate your power as a father or grandfather.* It's never too late to employ new ideas about fathering. You have time to work through these secrets carefully and systematically. But what you don't have time for is procrastination. Even if you start with only one secret, the important thing is to start *now.*

The second strategy for applying the secrets is to choose one secret to work on. Reread that chapter. Discuss it with your wife and your friends. Apply some of the practical tips that are included in each chapter.

Here we can take a tip from Pete Rose. Despite his gambling problems, Rose had a remarkable baseball career, eventually setting the league record for the most hits of all time. When asked to explain his success, Rose replied, "I practice what I'm not good at. Most folks practice what they're good at."[2] Rose looked at all the things that a baseball player is called to do, and he worked on one at a time. In addition, he singled out the areas of his greatest weakness and focused on them. Unfortunately, Rose did not apply the same principle to his family life. "When I was married, my wife said that I spent more time at second base than I did at home," he once remarked.[3] But Rose's principle of overcoming his greatest weakness is a good one for men wanting to improve their fathering.

Of the seven secrets, the one I have singled out in my own fathering as my greatest weakness (and the one I am devoted to working on at this moment) is the third secret—consistency. This is particularly true in relation to my eldest son, Joel, who has an incredible mind and memory for the words I say (perhaps because he himself is a man of few words). He hears the commitments I make (both explicit and implicit) and holds me to them. For example, one day I called him from work and told him that when I got home, he and I would play catch. When I did get

The Formula Father

He demands a home that is a model of order and discipline. Fathering consists mainly of a list of rules, a mechanical system that, he is convinced, will lead to success.

He lacks faith in his kids and allows them to make few of their own decisions. He also lacks faith in God; he has everything under control on his own.

The Faithful Father

Loyal: in the same way that a husband and wife pledge to be faithful to each other. The faithful father says, "My kids are a priority," even in the face of all the pressures and expectations the world places upon him.

Hard-working: like a good car. A lifelong commitment to keep plugging away at what he knows is sound fathering practice. He works hard at staying in touch with his kids, pressing on through the complexities and difficulties, focusing on his children.

Full of Faith: The faithful father does his duty, prayerfully, and trusts God for those things he cannot control

The Free-wheeling Father

He dwells on the fact that there are no guarantees his children will turn out OK, and the thought paralyzes him. His list is not a list of rules or desired results, but a list of all the things over which he ultimately has no control.

He defers to others when it comes to parenting responsibility (Go ask your mother). He doesn't realize that there *are* principles of fathering. He needs to do what he is able to do and trust the heavenly Father for the rest.

21

home, we did go outside, but instead of catch, I organized a game of kickball so that other kids, including the neighbors, could play. But Joel was disappointed. I had made a specific commitment (I had said *catch* and *he and I*), but I hadn't followed through.

It really troubles me when I find I am inconsistent toward my kids. But I try to be patient, and I tell myself that I'm working on it. I am committed to being a consistent dad as a first step toward being an effective dad. One step at a time. My good friend and fathering advocate Dave Simmons, who used to be a linebacker in professional football, tells the men at his fathering seminars: "Just run one play at a time."

The manner in which I am trying to become a more consistent father demonstrates the third way to apply the seven secrets. After you have gotten a general understanding of the secrets, after you have chosen one for particular focus, then commit to making that secret a point of interaction and accountability with your wife, family, and male friends.

Make yourself accountable to your wife. My wife, Dee, knows that I'm trying to work on consistency. In fact, she helped me identify consistency as an area to work on. And now she holds me accountable. For example, I made a commitment to take each of my children out to lunch once a month. With any family, but particularly a big family like mine, it's important to spend time with each individual and not just with your children all together. However, with five kids, it's sometimes hard to keep track of everyone. When the end of the month approaches, Dee helpfully reminds me which kids haven't had their monthly date with Dad. Dee also helps me set realistic goals so that my commitments are attainable. (In the spring of 1993, the National Center for Fathering will be releasing a book tentatively titled *Wives Helping Husbands Become Better Fathers.* Perhaps your wife can read this book and you two can make your fathering, and not only your parenting, a joint project.)

Make yourself accountable to your children. Sometimes there are ways you can bring your children into your work on

Survey Categories

Beginning in December of 1987, more than 4000 fathers have been surveyed concerning their fathering ideals and practices. More than 400 questions have been asked. In other samplings, both wives and adult children have also been surveyed concerning their husband's/father's performance. Scales with sets of questions were designed to identify particular areas significant to fathers. The following categories represent scales of questions with at least 2, but up to and including 41 questions per scale. The categories we surveyed included:

Involvement with children
Awareness of children's needs
Nurturance
Consistency with children
Motivation to father
Spiritual involvement with children
Time committed to children
Guilt associated with fathering
Involvement with discipline
Marital interaction
Involvement in education
Parental discussion relating to children
Dealing with family crisis
Showing affection/affirmation to children
Being a financial provider
Modeling
Freedom of expression in father/child relationship
Knowing your child
Satisfaction with his childhood
Satisfaction as a father
Satisfaction with support as a father
Satisfaction with leadership abilities
Satisfaction with verbal relationship with children

Parenting skills
Job satisfaction
Personal goals and hobbies
Planning family activities
Wife's commitment to mothering
Involvement in child's development
Verbal interaction between father and child
Expectations father has for the child
Planning child's future
Father's involvement in household's chores
Male identity issues
Parental confidence
Seeking outside advice/help
Being involved in child care
Extended family activities
Relationship with parents
Marital satisfaction
Parental satisfaction
Family life satisfaction
Time satisfaction
Satisfaction with father
Satisfaction with mother
Extrinsic religiosity
Intrinsic religiosity
Social desirability

23

one of the secrets. I asked my kids this morning to tell me about areas where I am consistent and where I am inconsistent. They said I am consistent in praying with them, in taking care of them, and in upholding the rules of the house, but that I am inconsistent in playing catch (there you go!) and in taking them out for ice cream. (OK, sometimes their insight is decidedly in their self-interest!)

Make yourself accountable to another father. Some of your best support in applying the secrets may come through other men. I get together informally with a fellow named Norm Wallace. He's twenty years older than I, and his kids are adults— he's experienced the full life cycle of fathering. Although Norm is always eager to give advice, he will also just listen while I talk about my kids. I have the opportunity to share about any struggles or frustrations, and he gives me the encouragement I need.

Make yourself accountable to fathering groups. The National Center for Fathering sponsors a number of fathering groups that meet in churches, homes, and communities across the country. Men get a chance to talk with each other about their fathering. A fellow in one of these groups once remarked, "You know, this is the only place I can come and admit that I've failed without being made to feel like I'm a failure." When we surround ourselves with other men and speak honestly before them, we gain their support and their accumulated wisdom. These men become fathering models for us.

All Your Children Really Need

A few months ago I met a man in Boulder, Colorado, who is a vice-president in a large corporation and the father in a small family. Doug was responsible for a great deal of the success of his company. He worked many long and productive hours. If he neglected his family in the process, it wasn't by conscious choice. He loved his wife. He loved his two sons.

In fact, when reports began to arrive from school that his oldest son, Mark, was having behavioral problems, Doug's love kicked into action. He resolved to do whatever it took to help his son.

Doug called around and found the most prominent child psychologist in the area. The doctor happened to be in south

---

Feedback on Fathering

Sometimes it is easy to be blind to our own strengths and weaknesses. The Lord has provided us with a spouse and with friends who can provide objective and caring insight into our fathering practices. Perhaps as a means to helping you identify which of the seven secrets should be the first one you work on, you can photocopy this worksheet and distribute it to your wife and those men who know you well. (If you are really brave, give a copy to each of your kids!)

1. In what area do you believe you excel as a father?

2. What one area of your fathering do you think requires the greatest improvement?

3. Please rank the following statements in the order that you believe they are true of you (1 being most true; 7 being least true):

- ☐ I maintain a high level of commitment to my role as a father.
- ☐ I know the unique characteristics of each of my children as well as what to expect from them at each growth stage.
- ☐ I am consistent toward my children when it comes to my words, moods, and behavior.
- ☐ I handle crises in a profitable manner and provide sufficiently for the financial needs of my home.
- ☐ I work diligently toward nurturing a strong marital bond with my wife.
- ☐ I actively listen to my children and allow them to express their thoughts, emotions, and concerns.
- ☐ I directly engage in equipping my children spiritually through teaching and modeling prayer, Bible study, and worship.

25

Denver, but Doug took time off work to make the hour's drive with Mark down to the appointment. He considered the rather exorbitant fees to be a small sacrifice for his boy's well-being.

Doug was sitting in the waiting room, flipping through the remainder of a tattered magazine, when Mark and the psychologist stepped out from their second appointment. Doug looked up expectantly. This doctor was one of the best in his field and would no doubt be formulating an elaborate but insightful diagnosis of Mark's problems.

Insightful, yes. Elaborate, no.

"All your son really needs," the highly trained professional said, "is a father."

Doug was ready to complain, "But he has a father," when suddenly the words sunk in and he knew. "My son needs *me.*"

The drive back to Boulder that afternoon was silent—not because of tension or embarrassment or shame, but because Doug was so busy thinking and feeling and planning and praying. When they arrived home and Doug opened the front door for his son to walk in, Mark entered a home that had just radically changed because of the commitment his father had made: *If my children need a father, then it is a father they will have.*

It is in the soil of such a heart that the seven secrets of effective fathers grow and prosper and shape the generations.

Three

SECRET 1: Commitment

Oliver DeVinck was just three months developed in his mother's womb when his mother had an accident. Gas leaked from the coal-burning stove in the kitchen. In the bedroom Catherine DeVinck lost consciousness, falling onto the bed. Oliver's father had already left for work, but at the train station he remembered something he had forgotten from home, and he returned to the house. José DeVinck immediately smelled the gas and quickly carried his pregnant wife outside into the fresh air.

She revived quickly. When Oliver was born six months later, he appeared to be a healthy baby boy.

A couple of months after the birth, Catherine was playing with Oliver before an open window. She held him up to the warmth of the bright sun, enjoying the fresh air and the sun's soothing rays. Then she noticed something odd. Her baby was staring directly into the sun without blinking.

Oliver was blind. Eventually the doctors would tell the DeVincks that Oliver not only couldn't see, he also wouldn't be able to hold up his head, crawl, walk, speak, or hold anything in his hand. The gas that Catherine had inhaled early in her preg-

29

nancy had affected Oliver's development. He was born with severe brain damage.

The DeVincks asked the examining physician what they might do for their son. The doctor suggested they place him in an institution.

José and Catherine refused to consider such a possibility. "He is our son," José said. "We will take Oliver home."

"Then take him home and love him," the doctor replied.

They did. For thirty-three years.

Even as an adult, Oliver was the size of a ten-year-old. He had a large head and twisted legs and required care for all of his thirty-three years. He was fed by his family three times a day. He was bathed and changed regularly. He was in all respects, as his younger brother Christopher would write, one of the "weakest, most helpless human beings" you would ever meet.

Christopher DeVinck once asked his dad, "How did you manage to care for Oliver for thirty-three years?"

"It was not thirty-three years," his father replied. "I just asked myself, 'Can I feed Oliver today?' and the answer was always, 'Yes I can'."[1]

Oliver DeVinck died in 1980 and was buried in Weston, Vermont.

We can learn a lot about commitment from dedicated fathers such as José DeVinck. Even though most of us don't face the challenge of caring for a handicapped child, the task seems hard enough with healthy children. José DeVinck models for us the first secret of effective fathers: The effective father is one who maintains a long-term commitment to his children.

Claiming Your Children As Your Own

José DeVinck stood up and said, "He is our son."

He is your son. She is your daughter. Will you claim them as your own? Will you give them your name? Will you declare to them and others that your futures are bound up together?

We're amused by the enthusiasm of the father who jumps up

COMMITMENT

A father's commitment to his children is demonstrated by his readiness and willingness to carry out his fathering responsibilities. Is he eager to be with his kids? Does he enjoy the fact that he is the one they're depending upon? Or does the "responsibility" intimidate him to the point where he dreads his fathering duties and procrastinates?

When strong fathers were compared to other fathers, these comparative scores resulted:

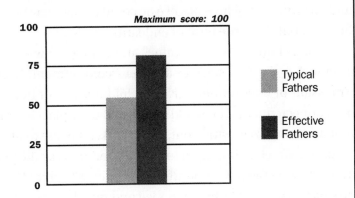

The strong fathers as a group scored 77% of the maximum on the commitment scale, compared to 59% for the typical fathers. Practically speaking, an effective father answered "good" on questions related to his commitment level, while a regular father answered "fair." Of all the seven secrets, the difference in the commitment scores (between effective and typical fathers) were the greatest. Effective fathers scored 30% higher than typical fathers.

in the middle of a Little League game, points to his son rounding third base, and yells, "That's my son!" The kid may turn red, but I suspect the child is flushed with more than just embarrassment. He probably feels a rush of pride.

Kids need us to claim them as our own.

Here in Kansas, when you go pheasant hunting, you have to stop at the farmer's house first to ask permission to walk his fields. The farmer will likely be in the shed working on some piece of rusty equipment. As you pull up into the driveway, he'll look up. Eventually he'll walk out to meet you. He'll rub his greasy hands off on an equally greasy rag and then shake your hand and introduce himself. Then invariably he'll nod his head over his left shoulder and say, "This's my boy, Jim." In some ways, it's not even an introduction—it's a claim, a fact of the universe. This "boy" may actually be a strapping twenty-two-year-old hunk of farm stock who looks like he could throw a hay bale over the barn, but that's the term of endearment: "My boy."

Telling children "you are mine" and telling the world "they are mine" is the first stage of a father's commitment. Such an expression of commitment gives a child a sense of belonging and connectedness. The world's a big and busy place. Adults of all shapes and sizes swirl about, off to work, off to the mall, off to the grave. Watch a little child in a crowd, perhaps as the people swarm toward the ticket counter at a basketball game. The little kid's hand grabs his father's pant leg and bunches the fabric up into his tiny fist so that his fingers are close to his father's leg. That fistful of pant leg is a point of reference, a connection with the one to whom the child belongs.

Fathers who tell their kids "you are my children" give them an invaluable point of reference. Children then feel secure in exploring the world because they always know where home is. They know where they belong.

Being claimed by one's father also gives a child a sense of affirmation. We all know how much rejection there is in the world, even for children. Some of us may still remember getting picked last for softball. It's a traumatic experience. Team captains don't even use your name or point to you as an individual. They say, "OK, I'll take these two. You take those two." You lose your identity. Or else, worse yet, the captains negotiate: "I'll take him, but only if you spot me three runs." You become a commodity to be dealt and traded. With so much rejection waiting up ahead, what a pleasure for a child to grow up in an atmosphere of early acceptance in which he hears his father say, "This is my son. He's on my team."

Making this claim communicates belongingness, acceptance, and pride to children, but it also communicates much to the father himself. When you say to your kid, "You are my child," you are identifying yourself with that child. You are raising the stakes. You are saying to yourself that you are willing to invest a good deal of your own prestige and happiness in how this child turns out. You are even willing to let yourself be embarrassed by that child on occasion. In a very real sense, your name is on the line. Now, we all know fathers (formula fathers) who carry this too far. They live their lives through their children pushing them to impossible achievement. Their love is conditional and based on performance. You hear them say, "I want you to do what I've never done." Or else they govern their children rigidly, anxiously battling any spot or blemish. Their selfishness is evident when you hear them say, "How could you disgrace *me* like this?" But these are formula fathers. Faithful fathers use this sense of identification merely to help fuel their motivation. The thrill of what's personally at stake propels them to do their best in the fathering task.

When you say to your kids, "You are my children," you are also claiming responsibility for them. It creates in you a sense of duty. As any good soldier or good fire fighter can tell you, a sense of duty can help you beat incredible odds. What keeps a sentry at his post when the temperature dips toward zero? What sends a fire fighter into a burning building after a trapped victim that he doesn't even know? A sense of duty can help you stick it out with a rebellious, drug-addicted, spiteful teenage child at a time when you look in your heart and find it difficult to locate any affection for him. "What made you stick it out?" someone might later ask you, and you would respond, "What'd you expect? I'm a father and that's what fathers do."

33

Resolving to Act As Your Child's Father

Commitment involves more than claiming your child as your own. It also requires you to choose to be your child's father, resolving to work for your child's benefit.

José DeVinck said, "We will take Oliver home."

Every year, parents of physically impaired newborns are called to make a difficult choice. Some parents agonize and come to the legitimate conclusion that an institution might best serve their severely impaired child's needs. The DeVincks made a different choice. The rest of us can learn a valuable lesson. Implicit in the DeVincks' choice to take Oliver home was also the choice not to leave him at the institution. The DeVincks understood that in one way or another Oliver would be fathered; the only question was by whom. Nurses at the institution could have fed him his daily supper of a poached egg mixed with cereal, warm milk, sugar, and a banana. An orderly could have come in regularly and changed Oliver's diapers. The federal government could have subsidized Oliver's upkeep. But no—DeVinck decided that *he* would do the boy's fathering.

As fathers we need to understand that if we choose not to actively father our children, someone else will. The world is filled with father substitutes—surrogates all too ready to step into the role:

1. **The TV as father.** Television says, "I'll watch over your children for you. I'll keep them preoccupied while you do your work and live your life." Of course, not only is the TV father notorious for feeding your children huge portions of the wrong foods, but it is also quite hard of hearing. There will be times your kids will want and need to express what they're thinking, feeling, and imagining, but the TV father won't listen and can't respond.

2. **The public school system as father.** At some point during your children's education there may be a public schoolteacher who will say, "I'm qualified with degrees in biology and psychology. I should be the one to teach your children about sex." Of course, the schoolteacher father is not allowed to discuss sex in a context of love or marriage.

③ **The federal government as father.** Uncle Sam says to many dads, "I've got you covered. I can make sure your kids get enough to eat. I might even foot their college bill. You don't have to worry about that." This sounds too good to be true, and it is. Millions of children are supported by the federal government father while their natural father remains out of work, distant, and perhaps even absent.

④ **The boyfriend as father.** You'll never hear this surrogate father directly, but if you did he would say, "Look, you and I are both grown men, aren't we? And we both know that your daughter, like all daughters, longs for the love and acceptance of an older man." He would then offer to give your daughter the affection she needs from you, but when he says *love,* he may actually mean his own selfish hormonal drive.

Believe it, men. If we don't father our children, someone else will. However well meaning they may be, surrogate fathers will never be able to do as good a job as we can, even given our weaknesses and shortcomings. Part of the commitment of fathering is resolving as José DeVinck did to be our child's father, to say as he said, "I will take my child home." *I will father.*

Mr. DeVinck knew what it meant to take Oliver home. Implicit in his statement was caring for him. "Then take him home and love him," the doctor said. The DeVincks made a commitment to feed Oliver when he needed feeding, to bathe him when he needed to be bathed. The commitment was a resolve toward action. *I will do for you those things that fathers do for their children.*

Fulfilling Your Commitment Daily

Your fathering commitment goes beyond your personal decision and vow to be the father in your child's life. It requires action. It must be not only an inner act of the will, but also an outer expression of service. You must not merely make a commitment, you must keep it.

Acting on your claim to your child involves two things: A

35

father must do *all* the things that fathers are supposed to do. And he must do them for the entire *time* that fathers are supposed to do them. He embraces the entire range of fathering activities and holds them for the entire period of enlistment.

What if you were hiring an accountant at work who told you at the interview, "I'll be your accountant, but I'll only credit accounts. I refuse to debit any"? The books would be as unbalanced as his thinking. For almost a century, men have been looking at the list of all that a father is called to do and have essentially been telling their kids, "I'll take on these two roles here. I'll be your financial provider and your disciplinarian, but all this other stuff about being a spiritual equipper or role model you'll have to find elsewhere. That's just not me."

The faithful father does not pick and choose what roles to fulfill. In some ways, his only limitation is ignorance. He may not know all that he should do as a dad, but once someone tells him, he'll do it. Interestingly, from our research at the National Center for Fathering, we've found that one of the most vigorously committed groups of fathers is those men who themselves didn't have committed fathers. We call these "overcomer" fathers, or sometimes "compensatory fathers."[2] They are fathers eager to be the father they wish they'd had.

Committed fathers embrace all the fathering roles, whatever is required at any time in their children's lives.

They also do so for the long haul. Remember what José DeVinck said? "It was not thirty-three years. I just asked myself, 'Can I feed Oliver today?' and the answer was always, 'Yes I can.'"

Commitment involves the matter of time. Many fathers fudge on this. They put off their day-to-day involvement with their children with the idea they'll make a grand gesture later, a big commitment that will make up for their lack of regular commitments along the way. They talk about substituting quality time for quantity time. They buy their child an expensive ten-speed bike for Christmas. They focus on the big events in a child's life—birthdays, graduation, even marriage—to express their commitment. They may think of gifts of money or a child's inheritance as the measure of fathering commitment.

Real fathering commitment, however, is expressed in day-to-day activities. The word *commitment* in fact has a revealing etymology. It literally means to give, hand over, or entrust. When you "commit" something to memory, you give your memory the bits of information and trust that it won't forget them. The most helpful image here might be of the person who walks into a bank, digs in his pocket for the money he has wadded up there, and slides it under the glass window to the bank teller. He's making a deposit. He's committing his money to their safekeeping. → Examples:

Similarly, like a faithful bank customer, we need to make regular (daily) deposits into the lives of our children. What is it that we deposit? Time, energy, and resources. Commitment is the actual amount of time, energy, and resources you are willing to pledge to the task of fathering. Your daughter has a fever, and you stay beside her bed through the night, sleeping only in fits in an uncomfortable chair. You've made a deposit. Your son asks you, "Dad, how do you check the oil in a car?" and you grab a rag for him to use on the dipstick. You've made a deposit. You tie a shoe—money in the bank. You teach a prayer—your savings continues to grow.

While many of us may be waiting for that big ship to come in financially, all of us subconsciously know that the person who makes it big is the one who invests a little bit now, then a little later, and later, regularly putting some aside, making frequent deposits. However small each individual deposit might be, eventually it adds up to a huge investment account.

I have an irresistible urge to run this analogy into the ground. For instance, we could also talk about how the little deposits in our children's lives also accumulate interest (at double-digit rates!). Within their talents and imaginations and potentials, our small but regular bits of support and encouragement compound themselves into some mighty accomplishments. Bonnie Blair, the Olympic gold medalist mentioned

37

earlier, dedicated her medal to her father, who had died two years before. "He always used to tell me, 'You can do it,'" she said.[3]

Fathering commitment is best expressed in small but regular ways. A sixth grader wrote in an essay: "Awhile ago my father had picked me up from school after a stressful day and said to me, 'Sandy, one day I'll be a big star.' I turned to him and said, 'You'll always be a star to me, Daddy!'" This man was waiting and hoping for the one big moment when he could be everything he wanted to be for his child. He needed to be reminded, "Daddy, you're already a star to me. You're here, as you promised, to pick me up from school, and now look, here you are simply spending time with me." There is no need for this father to complain, "Oh, but those are such small things."

What is commitment as it applies to fathering?

It is claiming your children as your own.

It is resolving to act toward fulfilling the totality of your fathering role.

It is doing the day-to-day activities that fulfill your resolve.

How Effective Dads Approach Their Fathering Commitment

At the end of this chapter, I'll give you a means by which to measure your level of commitment as a father. I'll also give you a list of practical tips for raising and sustaining your commitment and motivation. But first, let's take our thinking one step further.

What makes the commitment of an *effective* father different from that of an *ordinary* father?

We have to admit that most of us are ordinary fathers. We may not be the best fathers in the world, we may not be effective fathers, but we still must be doing something right. We aren't absentee dads. We haven't abandoned our children. We put in hours fulfilling fathering duties.

Or do we?

± ll

Maybe not. Statistics show that children in the United States spend less time with their parents than children in any other country in the world. In the former Soviet Union, fathers on average spend more than two hours a day with their children.[4] Yet in the United States fathers spend as little as thirty-seven seconds a day with their young kids.[5] The amount of time says something about our commitment to the task. We spent more time winning the space race than we did the fathering race.

The facts state clearly that effective fathers quite simply spend more time with their kids than do ordinary fathers.

However, the commitment of effective fathers involves more than just the time clock.

Effective fathers pursue their commitment aggressively. They *think* about their commitment level. While other fathers may simply try to ward off thoughts of giving up and tossing in the towel, effective fathers consciously pursue commitment to their kids. Effective fathers *talk to their children* about their commitment. "I'm committed to you," they say. I know of one father who showed his son a piece of paper. "I want you to see this," he told the boy. "This is a list of my priorities. I wrote down everything that I felt called by God to do at this point in my life. I want to show you how high you and your mother fall on my list." Effective fathers *talk to others* about their commitment: "I made a commitment to my kids, and by golly, I'm not going to let this latest obstacle stand in my way." They *plan* their future commitment: *This year Susie goes to high school for the first time. She's going to need a lot of my strength. In fact, I'm going to resolve to get up an hour earlier each morning just so I can have a leisurely breakfast with Susie and help prepare her for the day.*

Effective fathers monitor their commitment level closely. They read their vital signs like a stockbroker reads the *Wall Street Journal* or like a presidential candidate reads the polls. Is my fathering getting crowded out by other activities? Am I reluctant to interact with my kids? Effective fathers examine their hearts regularly to see if they are still turned toward their children.

39

The effective father differs from other dads in that when he finds his commitment ebbing low, he actively seeks ways to stimulate it again. Most often he finds his encouragement from other fathers. He gets together with other men.

Fathering groups have been a great boon for my friend Larry Schafer up in Minnesota. He's been meeting with other men for five years now to specifically work on his fathering skills. What's comical is how his whole family has gotten behind him. Invariably one of his four children will ask him what he's learned in fathering group that week. Once, one of his boys reminded him, "Don't miss fathering group tomorrow." Apparently, the kids know the vested interest they have in their dad's meeting with other men.

Actually women have known this secret for years. When women get together for a cup of hot tea, and one of them chimes in, "You should have seen what that fool kid of mine did last Friday," they aren't griping about motherhood. They are sharing experiences and commiserating. They are swapping tips and telling each other, "Be encouraged, you are not alone." Women are wonderful at finding encouragement and support by gathering together. Men need to do the same.

Effective fathers have a *task orientation* toward their fathering. They view their fathering as an occupation ("this is what I do") and not merely as a circumstance ("this is what happened to me"). To an effective father the role is an occupation. To an ordinary father it's an obligation. It's like the difference between the employee who works hard to do a job well and the employee who simply puts in his hours.

good)

Effective dads view the word *father* as a verb, not just as a noun. It is possible "to father." You would be surprised how new this concept is. We've always talked about "mothering," but "fathering" is a new term on the block. (At the National Center for Fathering, we've seen this in response to our name. Phone callers have misunderstood us as "the National Center for Feathering" or—perhaps somewhat accurately—"the National Center for Bothering"!)

40

In research on gifted children, one of the striking findings is that, beyond their creativity and intelligence, they are task-oriented.[6] Gifted fathers are much the same. This task orientation enables them to take advantage of all the same resources that make for success in their jobs. Do you have goals at the office? Make goals at home and watch how that increases your motivation. Did you receive training for your profession? Then get training for your parenting: increase your skills, and watch how your confidence level increases. Do you have a network of co-workers and colleagues who support your efforts in your career? Then create a network that includes your wife, your pastor, and other men who will support you in your fathering commitment.

The effective father draws confidence from the role of father itself. In other words, he doesn't look solely at his own personal background, skills, and intellect, judging them to be inadequate for the task. Instead, he recognizes that there's a lot of power inherent simply in the position of father. Constitutional authority, if you will.

When Dwight Eisenhower reviewed his troops before the Normandy Invasion, he could have worried that one of his privates would suddenly step out of rank and say, "Hey, wait a second, you're just a farm boy from Abilene, Kansas. There's no way I'm going to let you tell me to hit that beach." Eisenhower may have thought about that, but I doubt it. He probably knew that the five stars on his helmet represented legitimate authority, giving him confidence to make the crucial orders to win the war. There is similar power inherent in simply being a dad. I assure you that more than one of the effective fathers we have studied have confessed a sense of personal inadequacy. Yet however inadequate they may feel, they have a great deal of confidence in fatherhood. The Father of all fathers established faithful fathering as one of his essential tasks. We can trust in his design and follow his example.

When the complexity of the task grows, so does the effective father's motivation. An effective father rises to meet the challenge. It's easy to be committed when all is smooth and

41

delightful. One morning, as you are in the bathroom shaving, you look down and there is your son beside you, with shaving cream also on his face, scraping it off with his plastic toy razor. You smile: it's good to be a dad. But twelve years later, you and he are at that same mirror. Now he's leaning over and pulling at his earlobe, trying to decide whether he should get it pierced and what kind of earring to wear. He no longer wants to be just like you. In fact, he's embarrassed when you walk up to him and his friends. It may just be a phase, but it's a painful and complex one, and the relationship is difficult. Nonetheless, a committed father responds, adapts, changes, meets the challenge. What keeps a man doing his job when the satisfaction seems so low? Part of it, no doubt, is the same heroic spirit that Teddy Roosevelt spoke about:

> It is not the critic who counts: not the man who points out how the strong man stumbled or where the doer of deeds could have done them better. The credit belongs to the man who is actually in the arena: whose face is marred by the dust and sweat. . . . Far better it is to dare mighty things, to win glorious triumphs even though checkered by failure, than to rank with those poor spirits who neither enjoy nor suffer much because they live in the gray twilight that knows neither victory nor defeat.[7]

But another part of this courage in the face of challenge is simply the recognition that *I'm a father and this is what fathers do. Just because circumstances have become more difficult does not mean that my responsibilities have changed.* Fathers father. Committed fathers do their duty. Effective fathers find ways to be effective in the face of adversity and discouragement.

Testing Your Commitment

How committed a father are you? One way to measure your commitment is to test yourself against the six commitment characteristics of effective fathers that we listed above.

1. Do you pursue your commitment aggressively, thinking about it and verbalizing it to your children?
2. Do you monitor your motivation level to see if your commitment is slipping?
3. Do you seek out resources to help you maintain your motivation, such as getting together with other fathers?
4. Do you consciously try to conceive of your fathering in task-oriented terms and apply the same standards of excellence in the home that you do in the office?
5. Do you draw confidence from your title and position as father?
6. Does your commitment and motivation rise when you encounter fathering challenges?

Another way to get feedback on your commitment level is to run yourself through our three-part definition of fathering commitment:

1. Have you consciously and verbally claimed your children?
2. Have you consciously and verbally resolved yourself to action on their behalf?
3. Are you regularly investing your time, energy, and resources in their lives, in a proportion fitting their high place on your list of priorities?

That last question is the rubber-meets-the-road test. Time is probably the most important indicator of commitment. Time spent with father is one of the most important needs of a child. You ask a kid how to spell *love* and he'll spell it T-I-M-E. It's such a scarce commodity in our busy culture. It is precious, a fleeting resource. Where we choose to spend it as fathers reveals a great deal about our true priorities. Please don't misunderstand. I'm not saying that those fathers who cannot spend time with their children because of outside circumstances are not committed. A better test would be to ask yourself this: If you were given a gift of one week of no responsibility, how would you spend that week? Would one of your focuses be activities with your chil-

43

dren? Obviously, commitment is much more than spending time with your kids, but time is a good thing to evaluate as a measure of your commitment to your children.

Another way to measure yourself is to ask if you are looking primarily for mountaintop experiences with your kids, or whether you are doing the daily chores necessary to build them up regularly. Specifically, ask yourself about your involvement in your children's education. The effective fathers that we sampled seemed to be particularly committed to their children's education.

Strengthening Your Commitment Right Now

Regardless of what you consider your present level of commitment, there are some practical activities we can all do to strengthen our commitment to our kids.

Verbalize your commitment to your kids. Tell them that they are important to you. Tell them that you are committing yourself to be the best father you can be for them. Write a letter to your kids. I assure you that letter will be read and reread; it may get packed in their bags when they go to college; it will get pulled out of the drawer when they are adults.

Share your childhood with your kids. My friend Brian chose the Christmas season one year to do this. His father passed away a few years ago. But last winter Brian took his family back to his hometown to see relatives his kids knew only through pictures. Brian took his daughter and son into the musty, run-down homestead. He walked them through each room and told them stories of Christmas trees his father brought home that were too big to fit through the door. He remembered the glittering star that only his dad had been tall enough to place on top of the tree. Each room had memories, including his own bedroom, where his father used to kneel each night to pray with Brian before he went to sleep.

It was in that bedroom that Brian turned to his kids. His voice was soft, but full of resolve: "Kids, what I remember most about the holidays is that my dad was there. Nothing spectacular, he was just there." He paused, and began again: "Ashley and John, I haven't been there for you like my dad was for me, and this year I want to make you two a top priority."

Brian's kids nodded approvingly. Though they could never articulate it, somewhere deep inside of them they had waited for this, listening for these words more eagerly than they had ever listened for the sounds of Santa's reindeer on the roof.

Let your kids know you are accessible. When your son leaves for school, give him your phone number at work to put into his notebook. Tell him, "Son, I want to be there for you even when you are away at school. If you ever need me, give me a call."

Assist your children in the activities they enjoy. When your daughter is trying out for the school play, verbalize your commitment by saying, "Honey, let me know if you want me to read the other parts in the script so that you can memorize your lines."

Think of all the different places your child goes, think of all the different activities she does, and then try to place your commitment into each of those things. What you will have done is to place bookmarks in your child's life that, however confusing the plot might become, she can always find and refer to and know where she is. What you will have done for yourself is to open your eyes to all the wonderful opportunities you have to practice your fathering.

Notify others besides your children of your commitment to your kids. Pray to God and tell him of your intentions to be a better father, asking him to work through you to fulfill your commitment. Tell your wife, your friends, and the people you work with. This may feel a little strange, but it will yield some good results. For one thing, it will put you on record and make you accountable to others. Knowing that people are watching to see if you fulfill your commitment will make it seem more urgent that you do. Another benefit is that, assuming these people agree with your commitment, they will also do their part to

45

protect it. They will be reluctant to place demands on you which they think will distract you from your declared priorities.

Take advantage of events in your life as a father *where motivation is naturally high to reaffirm your commitment.* One of the most encouraging developments for fathers in recent years is the invitation men have received to join their wives in the birthing room for the delivery of their child.

When Nancy Swihart was in labor with her first child twenty-two years ago, her husband, Judson Swihart (one of my colleagues), called the hospital from the house and was told to bring Nancy in. The couple was met at the outside door of the hospital by a nurse; Judd was told to go home and wait for the doctor's phone call. He did. Two years later, their second child was born. This time, Judd was allowed into the waiting room, where he could pace back and forth with other expectant fathers. It wasn't until their third child was born some years later that Judd was finally allowed into the birthing room. Even then he was told, "Don't touch anything."

Today, the progression is complete. Fathers not only are allowed into the birthing room, but also are considered valuable participants in the delivery process. The opportunity of becoming a father and witnessing the birth of your child is rare. Martin Greenberg uses the term *engrossment* to explain a father's feelings for the newborn experience.[8] If you and your wife are still having children, don't miss the opportunity to be in the birthing room. It will equip you with a large reservoir of motivation.

Look for other "fathering events" as well. Maybe it's a child's birthday; maybe a memorable family vacation; maybe a pleasant Father's Day celebration. Other major milestones might be a child's conversion or baptism, a child's first day at school, a child's first date, his or her graduation, his or her wedding. All of these are wonderful opportunities to stoke your motivational fires.

Use visual reminders of your children as checkpoints for your *commitment.* Bring a photograph of your kids or a piece of their scribbled and signed artwork to your office or shop. Display it in a prominent place, where it catches your eye throughout the day. In fact, place these reminders throughout your daily itinerary. How about taped to your locker door at the health club? Above your lathe in the wood shop? A picture that reminds you of your children or family will provide inspiration. And when your children come to your workplace to visit and see their pictures displayed for all the world to see, they will sense your commitment to them.

Surround yourself with some of the "trappings" of fatherhood. George Bush looks up from his desk in the Oval Office and sees the Official Seal of the Presidency of the United States. It reminds him of the authority inherent in his position. While there is no Official Seal of Fatherhood, it's fun to receive plaques and coffee mugs and sweatshirts which proclaim that you are a dad and that fathers are respected.

Look for occasions (even create them) where you can simply have fun with your kids. Part of sustaining our motivation at work is taking those two weeks of vacation a year. You need to take a vacation as a father. But take a vacation from the seriousness of your task, not a vacation from your kids themselves. Simply make time to enjoy the good gifts God has given you.

Four

SECRET 2: Knowing Your Child

I don't do much gardening, but a pastor friend of mine loves the hobby. Part of the fascination, Steve explained, is knowing how to do it. "You see," he said, "if you're planting tomatoes, you're after the fruit; if you're planting broccoli, it's the leaf you're interested in; if you plant carrots, it's the root." He went on to explain the importance of this knowledge: "This will tell you which fertilizer to add to which plant," he said. "Otherwise you might get carrots with giant leaves but no root, or tomatoes with deep roots but no fruit."

My friend Steve applies the same painstaking study to his family and his church. Not only is he a good gardener, he's a good shepherd. He calls the sheep of his flock (that is, his wife, his two daughters, the members of his congregation) *by name*. He knows them—their strengths and weaknesses, their hopes and aspirations, their joys and sorrows—and is able to minister to their needs. His family and his church (and his garden) flourish.

An effective father knows his children. He studies them and their world like a gardener studies a mulched garden. Part of his motivation is simple fascination: kids are amazing (and sometimes wonderfully funny) creatures. But an aware father also

51

wants to gain the knowledge necessary to cultivate his children's unique gifts and talents, while protecting his children from the dangers that his watchful eye detects. The second secret of effective fathers is *knowing your child.*

Knowing How the Garden Grows

There are two components to an effective father's knowledge of his child. One is a general knowledge of how *all* children grow and change. The other is a specific knowledge of who *his* children are as individuals. In other words, an effective father knows children (in general), but also knows his own children (in particular).

The technical term for a *general* knowledge of how children grow and change is *developmental awareness.* A developmentally aware father can tell you what to expect of children as they pass through different ages, stages, and phases. This developmental awareness might seem like so much book knowledge—something best left to child psychologists. But effective fathers actively seek out such knowledge. They watch other children and maybe their nieces and nephews. They quiz older fathers. They search their own childhood memory banks. They try to keep themselves informed about the different stages of childhood.

Each stage of a child's life blossoms with new activities, insights, and possibilities. The emotional, physical, mental, and spiritual aspects of their lives constitute a garden of potential. Your job as a father is to weed the garden and prepare the right amount of soil so that these flowers have full opportunity for growth. In order to do this, you must have knowledge of the soil conditions, the plants' needs, and what combination brings growth. Developmental awareness gives you this knowledge of the garden and the growth processes in life. While you may know that plants need water, developmental awareness tells you which plants need how much water how often.

KNOWING YOUR CHILD

The scale for "Knowing Your Child" was obtained by comparing fathers' scores in items such as the following:

- Knowing what children are capable of at a particular age.
- Knowing what they need for healthy growth, emotional stability, and intellectual development, and knowing specifically how to aid them in that growth.
- Knowing each child's individual tastes, goals, and abilities, and supporting each one in his or her unique characteristics.
- Having a good idea what concerns, problems, and questions a child would have growing up in this day and age.

The accompanying chart should help illustrate how strong fathers were different from other fathers in the category of knowing your child:

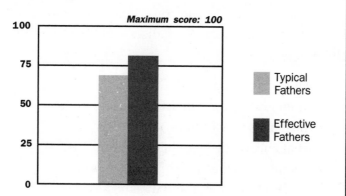

Typical fathers averaged 69% of the maximum score, while effective fathers averaged almost 19% higher than typical fathers. In practical terms, effective fathers felt that it was "somewhat true" that they knew their children. Typical fathers usually said they felt "undecided" or "unsure" about their knowledge of their children.

Tending to the Specific Needs of the Garden

Yet, what separates effective fathers from all other fathers is that they are also aware of who their children are as individuals. They know each child *specifically*. While a child progresses through the normal stages toward adulthood, he or she is developing also into a unique adult: a distinct person with his or her own set of personality traits, talents, strengths and weaknesses, likes and dislikes. Just as all snowflakes are white and frozen, but still no two are alike, so children may all be children, but again *no two are alike*. An effective father is aware of what makes his kid different from all the others on the block. Through the hospital nursery window, he may have been able to point through the glass and say, "That's my son there," because of the tilt of his ears or the birthmark on his cheek. And throughout life, an aware father can point and say, "That's my daughter. I can tell by the way she loves music, idolizes Amy Grant, averts her eyes when talking to boys, and fears getting called on in school." This man knows his child.

In our research on effective fathers, we discovered some specific things that effective fathers said they knew about their children:

- when his child had a difficult day
- when his child was upset about something
- the names of his child's best friends
- what encouraged his child the most
- when he had hurt his child's feelings
- his child's strengths and weaknesses
- what motivated his child
- when his child was embarrassed
- most of his child's recent disappointing experiences

Of course, this is not an exhaustive list of the information effective fathers want. These are indicators of a father who knows his children specifically, as individuals.

If your child grows up and one day becomes famous, you may wake up some morning and find reporters standing in your wife's flower beds. The doorbell rings, you are blinded by camera lights, and a microphone is stuck in your face. "Tell me about your kid. What was he like growing up?" But aware fathers aren't waiting for future biographers. Nor are they simply playing Trivial Pursuit. Effective fathers pursue knowledge about their children for two very important and immediate reasons: first, so that they can help create the conditions under which this unique personality (their child) can best blossom and prosper; and second, so that by recognizing danger signals they can alert themselves to situations where their children need their guidance and intervention.

My oldest daughter, Hannah, is a wonderfully gifted organizer. I am not. Hannah believes in a place for everything and everything in its place, while I am more naturally inclined toward a *pile* for everything and everything in its *pile*. But in my mind, unearthing Hannah's organizational skills is an important discovery. It will influence many of the things that I do with her as her father. For example, I consider this knowledge to be the seed of my counsel to her later in her career choices. She may grow up and find great fulfillment in being a charge nurse. On the other hand, she may want to become a librarian who will have all the books on the right shelves and the card catalog updated. She may want to become a corporate executive who is flown in to reorganize a company's structure and increase productivity. But it's unlikely that she'll be happy with the frantic pace of an air traffic controller or emergency medical technician. You see, I know her.

Knowing that Hannah is highly organized has also helped me govern my own behavior. I want Hannah to enjoy being at home. I want to insure that the environment she grows up in is positive and encouraging, that it is conducive to her growth. Consequently, I have made more of a point to be organized myself, adding, I hope, to Hannah's happiness.

One last example of the benefit of discovering Hannah's skills is that it has helped me become a better manager of the household. We know about management in the workplace: a supervisor organizes his personnel so they can accomplish their goals in the most efficient manner. Though you may never have thought of it before, a home can also have goals. A basic family goal is survival—keeping everyone fed, clothed, and sheltered. Another goal is growth and education: raising our kids (and ourselves) into mature, responsible adults. Outward goals may include service as a family to God and other people. A father, as the head of the household, needs to manage his resources to accomplish those goals. His most important resources are the other people in his family, including his kids. God knew what he was doing when he gave us the types of children he did. An effective father discovers what unique contributions each of his children can make to the family goals, and utilizes them efficiently. He sees the family as a divinely equipped team.

One child might enhance the family vacation by carefully watching the map and making sure the driver doesn't take the wrong roads. Another child might be the official photographer, because he or she has a keen eye for beauty. A third child might make the long hours in the car more enjoyable by telling some amazingly entertaining stories. When you know your kids, your team can function well.

Part of our basement is a play area with balls and toys and games, but another part is classroom space with a library, a chalkboard, and some desks. In an attempt to teach Hannah responsibility and to encourage her in her organizational gift, we've "given" her the basement. She keeps close track of our arts and crafts inventory and makes sure everything the family needs is at hand. She does a wonderful job.

Knowing who your child is helps you as a father create the conditions for your child to blossom into the uniquely beautiful adult God intends him or her to be.

The other main reason why effective fathers pursue knowledge of their children is to help them ward off things that might hurt their children.

One of the true pleasures in a Kansas gardener's life is sweet corn: big yellow ears with kernels that explode when

Awareness: Finding a Balance

HIGH

INTRUSIVE: Fathers who describe themselves as involved in every aspect of their children's lives may not allow their children much of a life of their own. The father's intrusion into every detail of his children's lives without consideration for their privacy or individualism can give his children little space to develop their own personality.

DISCERNING: Fathers in this group know not only what events are occurring in their children's lives; they also know how these events are perceived by each child. These fathers are able to discern their children's interpretations of the events in the context of their levels of development.

AWARE: This type of father has sufficient interaction with his children to know the particular needs, characteristics, and daily happenings of his children. These dads know the daily experiences of their children at home, at school, and in the community. They know what to expect from their children relative to each child's age group, and they know how their children compare with their peers. These fathers are aware of specific life events and are able to see some of the meaning these events have for their children.

UNCLEAR: Dads who depict themselves in this manner have some ideas about what is occurring in their children's lives, but these ideas are not specific. He does not know the details of his children's lives and would have difficulty naming his children's friends. These fathers most likely know about the more dramatic events their children experience, but not daily occurrences.

UNAWARE: In general, fathers who describe themselves as low in awareness are living in a world separate from that of their children. They often have little knowledge of the issues with which their children are dealing as well as having little knowledge about their children's school, friends, and personal experiences. These fathers may not be able to describe their children's uniqueness nor know what to expect from them relative to each child's age group.

National Center for Fathering (1990). *Personal Fathering Profile*, p.9.

LOW

57

you bite into them. Now a gardener might plant the seed and then hook up an automatic sprinkler system and even hire a neighbor kid to weed around the stalks, but he will still be down there each day looking at the plants and observing their growth. In particular, he's looking for holes in the leaves, which might indicate chinch bugs, and he's looking for black spots, which might indicate blight. He's gaining knowledge so he can take action when he needs to. When he spots a telltale sign, out comes the pesticide. A couple days before harvest, the gardener is back down at the garden, but this time he's looking around the edge of the garden too. He's looking for footprints—small five-toed footprints that give sign of the presence of that scourge of Kansas sweet corn: raccoon. Kansas coons also know sweet corn. When a gardener discovers that these bandits are afoot, he takes action to protect his crop. Some string up an electric fence, two strands high, with enough juice coursing through it to light a small town. I've also heard of some gardeners sleeping out in their gardens the night before harvest.

Effective fathers get to know their kids in order to come to their aid in moments of danger. Part of this preventive knowledge is awareness of a child's particular susceptibilities. Your child may seem more trusting than other kids. This trait can be a strength, as he is inclined to think the best of others, but it can also make him susceptible to being taken advantage of. If you know your child is naturally gullible, you can prepare him by discussing with him the types of people who are and aren't to be trusted. You would want to doubly emphasize that he is not to accept rides from strangers. Or maybe your child has a competitive streak. Again, this can be a strength, in that it will help her to excel, but it can also cause her to be a proud winner or poor loser. You would want to counsel her on respecting the feelings of others.

The Gardener's Pride and Joy

Being specifically aware of what is going on in our children's lives provides other benefits besides just helping us foster their growth and protect them against danger. When we show genuine interest in our children for who they are, we communicate that we consider them to be important and fascinating people. Regardless of how cruel and insensitive the school crowd might be, a father can make his child feel that "in this house, you are part of the in crowd." Through his inquisitiveness, a father tells his children, "I consider you worthy to be known."

Yet, children hear more than just the pride and affection that is communicated. Children sense security and confidence when their father puts a mark on the wall year after year to mark their growth. The child knows that her growth and development are being monitored by dad. Or children look eagerly at places where they have put their handprints in the wet cement of a new patio or driveway. This provides a reference point for them to return to in later days and say, "Look at me, I'm growing up."

A second benefit is that awareness helps relieve some of the unease we have as fathers. I know some dads who sit around waiting for the other shoe to drop. At any moment, they believe, their daughter could come home and say, "Dad, I'm pregnant." At any moment, they believe, they could get a phone call from their son: "Dad, come bail me out of jail. I got busted for possession." In some ways, these paralyzed fathers are right: at any moment, these things could happen, because they are unaware of the signs that they might happen. Aware fathers don't live with such a dread. They can see the storm on the horizon and take measures either to avert it or to weather it. They are not immune to tough times, but rarely are they surprised when bad weather blows in.

A third benefit of being an aware dad is simply the joy and fascination that knowing our children can provide. Let's face it: we have unique and interesting kids. These little human beings can provide us with an adventure of discovery and insight.

Practical Gardening Tips

What are some ways that we can become more specifically aware of each child's distinctiveness? Let me offer some practical suggestions:

Simply ask them questions. (Believe it or not.) I know I'm stating the obvious, but how would you get to know anyone you've just met? If you meet a new couple at church, you might invite them over for dinner. The conversation would be interspersed with questions: "So, where are you from originally?" "Tell me how you two met." "What kind of work do you do?"

Do the same with your kids. Take them out for a Coke, just to talk. Ask them, "So who's your best friend this year?" "Oh yeah, what do you like about her?" "When you and she are having your best times together, what are you doing?"

(Ask questions, but don't interrogate. Your children need to sense that you are not gathering this information so you can beat them over the head with it later. As they sense that you are genuinely interested in getting to know them, they will become more open and allow you greater access to their thoughts and emotions. But for now, if they don't volunteer information, don't force it out of them.)

Spend time on your child's turf. You will never fully understand or even believe some things unless you see them with your own eyes. Several years ago, when my daughter Sarah was seven, she took diving lessons. It had been some time since I had been with her at the pool, so I was caught a little off guard one evening around the supper table when my son Joel said, "Dad, you should have seen Sarah. She did a flip off the high dive."Yeah, right! I knew Sarah. There was no way she would even climb up to the high dive, let alone flip off of it. Sarah didn't say a word. I think I may even have accused Joel of lying.

The next week, I went to watch Sarah's diving class. Sure enough, there on Sarah's turf, amid the chlorine smell and the echoing cement, I gained insight into who my daughter is and how she thinks. All the kids were doing flips off the low dive. But Sarah had reasoned that if flips are possible on the low level, they

Knowing Children: Developmental Awareness

An effective father has a general awareness of how all children grow and change. There are charts that can help fathers map out and prepare for their children's development. These charts typically cover all aspects of a child's life (physical, emotional, social, intellectual, sexual, and spiritual) and all stages of development.

In one such chart, here is what appears under "Physical, Age 5":

> *Child can run, jump, climb. Learns to hop and skip this year. Child grows approximately 6 inches and gains about 10 pounds in weight. Can dress self, tie shoes, brush teeth, button clothes.*

Obviously, a father of a five-year-old should not expect his child to sit still for very long and would want to give him plenty of exercise. It would be a good time to start teaching grooming and health care, and with the way the child is growing, the father would need to budget for plenty of new clothes.

Benefits of Developmental Awareness:

1. *It's more likely that your child's needs will be met.* Awareness informs and focuses your fathering, so your efforts to create an environment of growth are not misdirected.

2. *Added fathering confidence and motivation.* Awareness is a foundation, a starting point when you don't know what to do. You have knowledge that is proven reliable; you're not shooting blindly or "just muddling through."

3. *Appropriate expectations.* As the world tells your child to "grow up" and "be a big girl," you know what she really needs, what behavior to expect, and how to encourage her without pushing.

Do Your Homework

Visit the local library and enlist help from experts on children. This will help you stay ahead of the game where your child is concerned. You'll be better equipped for your child's current stage, but you'll also be ready for what's coming in a few years.

Ask your wife. Seriously. She has endured nine months of extensive physical and emotional changes, and she's naturally keen to development. If you have daughters, your wife can help you understand the changes they're going through. Her perspective is invaluable.

Talk to older fathers. They've been there and back, and they'll be glad to share their war stories. Their insights will help you anticipate your child's stress points and respond with informed confidence.

Search your own memory banks. You were a kid once, with similar, though not identical, experiences. Just make sure you see how it really was instead of how you think it should have been.

Learn from your first child. Experience with one child will alert you to the changes that children go through, but remember that each child's reactions to those changes may be different. Children are not figures in a fathering formula; they're unique individuals.

Recommended Resources

John M. Drescher, *Seven Things Children Need* (Herald Press).

Paul Heidebrecht, *Time to Go Home* (Great Commission Publications).

Ask Yourself

How many of these statements can you agree with?

1. I have a good handle on the issues that my children face.

2. I understand the stages of child development.

3. I know what my child's emotional needs are at a given age.

4. I know what each child is able to do at his or her age.

5. I know how to teach my child personal responsibility.

must be even easier from higher up, where you have more room to flip around. I finally understood how adventuresome she really is.

Provide plenty of different opportunities for your child to discover her interests and talents, and for you to discover them too. Sarah enjoyed diving class until the instructor began working on her flipping technique. The moment she got some training, my daughter, who could do flips off the high dive, was suddenly doing bellyflops off the low dive. She lost interest. Since then she's explored other interests: piano, violin, ballet, gymnastics, pantomime, and boys. Multiply all these activities by five kids and you can guess that I'm a typical dad—busy. My wife drives kids to gymnastics, where I pick them up to take them home. And then there are times when I have to make the tough decision between being at Hannah's recital or Joel's T-ball game.

When the children are young, it's good (though expensive) for them to have variety in their activities. They are sorting out what they are good at and what they like to do (which are invariably the same). Eventually the barrage of activities will lessen, and you will have plenty of time to teach them about responsible commitment to a few activities. The big key is not to hammer your kids. Don't put them into the Olympic training mode. The goal for both you and them is *discovery, not performance.*

Give your child feedback about what you observe, particularly when that feedback is praise. "Wow, your sketching looks nice. Watching you draw it, I could tell you were really enjoying what you were doing." Not only does feedback provide a good opportunity for you to encourage your kids, but it also allows them to affirm or correct your observations, and you find out a little bit more. "Yeah," your son might say, "I like drawing with charcoal, but I think watercolor is what I'm really good at."

Get a different angle on your child by listening to your wife, your other children, his teachers, and his coaches. At any one time, you only see part of the picture, if that. When you look at an object, you only see the part facing your direction. In the

63

1700s William Whately commented that in parenting "two eyes see more than one."[1] Your wife is that other eye. And of course, she is as keenly interested in the children as you are. Ask her what she has observed. Along with telling you her perceptions of the kids, she can also give you feedback about your relationship with each of them as a father (something it is easy for all of us to become blind to). Father and mother are a parenting team.

There are also other eyes you can look through. Don't wait for the next parent-teacher conference; call up your child's teacher and ask for a progress report. Ask not only about grades, but also about how your son or daughter is interacting with the other students. Coaches are also good sources of information. If it's a team sport, they are constantly evaluating strengths and weaknesses to determine how each player can best benefit the team. And don't forget the reports of other children. On occasional evenings around the dinner table we have each family member say what he or she likes best about each other family member.

When it comes to drug use, be careful not to assume that your children are different from other children. When the drug movement spread through Johnson City, it was the talk of the town. My friend Dave was one of the men who would meet in the coffee shops and barbershops and swap stories about which kids had recently been picked up for drug possession. One teenager was found wandering around the city park chasing imaginary lions as the result of a trip on LSD. The men Dave was with even laughed about this boy's antics. Though the school administration was trying to deal with the problem, most fathers in the community, Dave included, never stopped to consider that their son or daughter might be involved. They simply didn't know what was going on in their children's lives.

Dave was a busy man. He was a real-estate agent who managed a number of listings. He was a good provider and disciplinarian for the family. His had all the makings of a successful family. But Dave had little specific knowledge of his son. Perhaps he was too busy at work or didn't know how to deal with the issues confronting his son John. After all, drugs were not around when he was growing up. Whatever the situation, Dave never asked John about the drug situation at school, and it was three years after John started using drugs regularly that Dave found out his son was addicted to cocaine!

If Dave had sought to know his son's difficulties and the struggles with self-identity that led the boy into the drug culture, it might have saved fifteen years of John's life—the time it finally took him to kick the drug habit.

Don't assume your children are different from other kids when it comes to sexual activity. You may be aware of the statistic that by age eighteen, 43 percent of churched youth have experienced sexual intercourse, but are you open to the possibility that your own son or daughter might be among that number?[2]

A friend of mine was the chaplain at a private university in the Midwest. As the chaplain of this conservative school, he provided counseling for the students. One year, he had counseled twenty female students who had come to him with problems related to being involved sexually with their boyfriends. When he began to inquire about their sexual involvement, he quickly found out that all twenty coeds had had no real relationship with their father. All of them described their father as either absent or distant.

Another friend of mine who was an exemplary leader of youth was dumbfounded when his daughter called one day to tell him that she was pregnant. He had given scores of talks about sex to other adolescents, yet he had somehow failed to know that his own daughter might need his help in this area.

Please don't misunderstand this section. I am not saying you need to control your children's sex life. Rather, you are to help them understand the way they are made and that the gift of sexuality has a positive expression in the marriage relationship.

Knowledge of your child's sexuality need not involve the crude and direct question, "So, are you sleeping around?" Neither does knowledge of the drug culture mean an automatic confrontation with your kids: "Are you using drugs?" If you have not shown interest in their lives up to this point, it's likely that your kids will clam up and even lie in the face of such accusatory inquiries. Knowledge of your children in these two vulnerable areas means knowing what they are thinking and feeling about these issues. Discuss drugs and sex with your kids early on. Be open. Let them ask you questions. Also be knowledgeable of the conditions in your children's lives that might make them particularly susceptible to drug use or sexual activity. Do they succumb too easily to peer pressure? Are they looking for escape or affection? (Treat the causes, not the symptoms.) And of course, be knowledgeable of their friends. Bad company corrupts good morals.

Resist focusing on one particular thing. Keep scanning; avoid staring. An airplane pilot has to do a number of things at the same time. He must constantly adjust the rudder pedals with his feet. With one hand he holds the wheel of the plane; with the other he adjusts the throttle. With his ears he listens to the radio. With his eyes, he is constantly checking the map and scanning the instrument panel. When a father forgets to scan, he faces the danger of getting caught in the same trap that a new pilot would fall into if he checked only the artificial horizon gauge. If a pilot looks only at the one gauge he may ignore his fuel level or his oil pressure, or icing on the plane, and get into serious trouble.[3] In the same way, don't assume that school is the only place where the action is for your child. Don't assume that just because Jenny is your daughter's best friend she's your daughter's *only* friend. Bits of knowledge about the whole range of your child's life are more useful to you as a father than in-depth knowledge about a few areas.

Be interested in your kids, but don't be intrusive. Perhaps you've been waiting for me to make this statement all chapter long. It certainly is important. In all my comments on knowing your child, I am not suggesting that a father become a private eye and monitor every move his children make.

In developing a perspective of awareness, picture a continuum that extends from being unaware of your children to the opposite extreme of being intrusive. The father who is unaware is living in a separate world from that of his kids. This is a free-wheeling father who has abdicated his role. On the other end of the continuum is the formula father, who does not respect his child's privacy. When he asks questions, the child senses that the father is not really interested in him as a person, but is checking up on him to make sure he isn't stepping out of line. For a faithful father, questions are a matter of interest; for a formula father, questions are an instrument of control.

As sure as the sun shines (and the rain falls and the rototiller revs), my next-door neighbor will be pounding on my back door in August with an armful of produce. He is an enthusiastic gardener, and my family is one of his main beneficiaries. "Look at these cucumbers," he says with as much pride as a father showing pictures of his children.

I'm afraid I don't get quite as excited as my neighbor does about cucumbers or tomatoes or zucchini, but it is an impressive sight—the fruit ripening on the vine. In the same way, every day I see some wonderfully beautiful children growing up around me, in homes of my friends, in our churches and communities. I ascribe the success to the same skill: careful knowledge of our children as we till the gardens of their lives.

Five

SECRET 3: Consistency

Long ago there lived the world's first mapmaker. I imagine he was someone who stepped outside the door of his home one morning, looked around, and said, "You know, this is a pretty big place." He may have been intrigued by the vastness and variety of the landscape and resolved to understand more fully where he lived. On the other hand, he may have simply been tired of getting lost all the time. For whatever reason, he decided to put it down on paper (or animal skin or tablets of stone). He was the world's first mapmaker, a prehistoric Rand McNally.

The world's first mapmaker had to start from scratch. If you were producing the world's first map, where would you begin? You would choose a point of reference and sketch out everything else from there. "OK, from here, it's twenty paces this direction until I hit a tree. It's fifteen paces this way, and I hit a rock. It's 245,000 paces this direction, and I hit Beijing." Pretty soon, constantly referring to the reference point, you get the whole earth mapped out.

This process makes the initial reference point a pretty important item. What if the world's first mapmaker chose an animal—for example, a woolly mammoth—as his reference point?

After all, a mammoth is certainly visible from a distance and a memorable landmark. But a woolly mammoth fails as a reference point because it isn't fixed; it's inconsistent. The creature may have stood there calmly underneath that tree when the world's first mapmaker started his map, but now it's off grazing in another field. The mapmaker tries once more, again using the woolly mammoth as his reference point, but then the animal saunters over to the foothills of a mountain, sunning itself by the rocks. Before long, the world's first mapmaker is confused, frightened, and, worst of all, *lost.* When he reaches what should be Beijing, he finds himself in Schenectady, New York.

Fortunately the world's first mapmaker chose a fixed, consistent point as his reference. In fact, he probably chose the front door of his own home. Home is where he always wants to be able to find his way back to. As long as he knows where home is, he can have the confidence to go out and explore the vast, unknown world.

The greatest explorers that this world has known are not David Livingstone and Christopher Columbus. The greatest explorers in the world live right under your roof. They're your children.

We talk about how children are natural explorers. Get my son Joel near a drainage culvert, and we may as well be at Carlsbad Caverns. He comes into the house and asks my wife for a flashlight, twenty-five feet of rope, and provisions for three days and two nights. But forget continents and caverns and mountains and moons: *all of life is uncharted territory for a child.* Everything is new and undiscovered. A newborn explores breathing, of all things. Walking is a new phenomenon. English is a foreign language even to an American, if that American is six months old.

After a while, the experiences will begin to accumulate, and the novelty will wear off. By the time the young explorer enters kindergarten, he won't even think about breathing or walking or speaking or the color yellow or the taste of peanut butter or the feel of his bed sheets. He has those items mapped out. But he is

CONSISTENCY

For an assessment of consistency, fathers were surveyed about whether they were regular or unstable in their behavior patterns, even-tempered or ever-changing in their emotions, and predictable or erratic in how they treated their children. The test results are represented by the following graph:

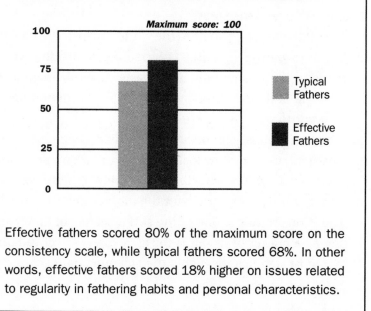

Effective fathers scored 80% of the maximum score on the consistency scale, while typical fathers scored 68%. In other words, effective fathers scored 18% higher on issues related to regularity in fathering habits and personal characteristics.

still constantly pushed to the edge of his map and barraged by new phenomena and experiences. He explores sitting in a classroom, obeying other adults, the politics of the playground. He explores addition and subtraction, his first loose tooth, his first crush. There's a lot of inner territory to discover too. What does it mean to be angry or sad or in love? He will eventually explore his belief system and try to discern whether there is a God and what to do with this person Jesus Christ that he keeps hearing about. Only an adult can understand Solomon's words, "There is nothing new under the sun." For a child, everything is new. They are discovering the world for the first time. They are the world's first mapmakers.

I don't know what granule of knowledge God gives a newborn. Maybe there are a few bytes of data programmed into our genes, and God says, "Here, start with this." It's more likely that God gives us not knowledge, but mapmaking abilities. Each child is born with the basic skills to begin mapping out his world, making sense of it, and living within it. We should not be surprised that these little mapmakers begin where all mapmakers begin: with a reference point.

A child's reference point in the world, the place from which he begins to map out his entire universe, is obviously his parents. It is crucial that his parents be consistent people: regular and predictable in their person and their actions. Children need to know what to expect—where they can find you—and this applies to your moods, your behavior, and your schedule. If you are inconsistent, they become lost in a large and frightening world.

In a sense, which we will discuss shortly, it is even more important for the father than for the mother to be a consistent person. Consistency is one of the seven secrets of an effective father. As a matter of fact, it is the area where effective fathers scored most significantly higher than all other dads.

The Consistent Father

Consistency, briefly defined, is *regularity* and *predictability.* When a child of a consistent father interacts with his dad, the child knows what to expect. There are few surprises and no scares.

An effective father is consistent in his person and in his actions. A consistent father governs his moods. He is not affectionate one minute and angry the next, with no indication that the tide was about to shift or no reason for the sudden mood swing. Inconsistent fathers are emotionally erratic. Years later, their children will stand up and confess, often through tears, "Whenever I approached my dad, I had no idea whether he was going to hug me or belt me." Passive-aggressive fathering is what we need to avoid.

A consistent father also governs his behavior. At the bottom line, this means that his children can count on his always being their father, always coming back home. Children of an inconsistent dad live with the threatening sense that their father's bags are packed and waiting by the door. They fear that one day their dad might rise from the dinner table, place his napkin down by his plate, and announce, "I'm leaving forever. Good luck and good-bye."

Not so with a consistent father. Children of a consistent dad know that when their father leaves for work with a kiss and a "See you later," he means just that. "I'll be back."

He also governs his behavior by practicing what he preaches. When he makes a promise, his children can count on his keeping it. In the movie *Hook*, Robin Williams, the successful Wall Street lawyer, who happens to be an inconsistent father, turns to his son and says, "When we get back, I'll go to all the rest of your games. I promise. My word is my bond." His son, the victim of numerous broken promises, replies, "Oh, yeah. Junk bonds."

An effective father does not make promises he cannot keep, and the promises he does make he fulfills. He also practices what he preaches by being consistent in his moral behavior. He does not say one thing and do another. He avoids hypocrisy at all costs. If he preaches to his kids about lying, he doesn't turn around and cheat on his tax returns. If he gets up at his daughter's wedding reception and proposes a toast to the sanctity of marriage, he does not sit back down and immediately start plotting an affair with the pretty woman he noticed sitting three tables over.

Consistency of Time

These elements of consistency may not surprise you, but let me tell you of another consistency characteristic that shows up in effective fathers. You may never have thought of it before, but children long for consistency in a father's schedule and daily habits. At any time during the day, regardless of where they themselves might be, children like to know where their fathers are and what they are doing. This is where fathers who are hourly workers may have an advantage over fathers who are entrepreneurs.

My own dad was an hourly worker at a factory. When it was 6:30, off he went to work. When it was 4:30, I knew that car pulling into the driveway was his. You may never have considered the act of getting up when your alarm clock rings every morning to be a habit that pleases your children, but it is. Consistency also applies to a father's hobbies and interests. There is something unsettling about a father who suddenly sells all his woodworking equipment so that he can take golf lessons for a month, before suddenly discovering that his "real" interest is monster truck rallies.

Children need consistent fathers. Now, you may accuse me of arguing for dull, routine, stuck-in-a-rut fathering. You may think our effective fathers are a bunch of fuddy-duddies. Well, so be it. If our children need dull fathers, let's be dull fathers. But I'm not arguing for dullness; I'm arguing for consistency. One child says, "Yeah, my dad is so much fun. We get together for family dinners and he's always got something up his sleeve. We're always surprised." But notice that this lively, enjoyable dad is also consistent. He's consistently there for family dinners, and yet he's also consistently fun. He's not boisterous at one dinner and then grumpy at others. His surprises are always pleasurable ones, not bombshells like "I'm leaving." His children know what to expect: a fun time on a regular basis.

Father, Child, World

When you talk about consistency, you actually have three entities involved, not just two. You are talking about a father, a child, and the world.

Picture a compass—the kind of compass you would use to draw a circle. One leg of the compass stands firm at some fixed point at the center of the page. It does not move. Oh, it will certainly lean toward the other compass leg as that leg moves further out from the center, but the foot of the central leg remains firmly planted. In our analogy, this central leg is the father. The other leg is where the action is taking place. It is out there moving around the piece of paper, drawing its line, circumscribing and exploring. It's rarely in the same place twice. At one moment, it's at the top of the paper and at the next it has swooped down to the bottom. But this leg of the compass is not moving erratically. It is drawing a carefully defined circle. The radius is constant, the arcs match, the sines and cosines are easily computable. When the leg comes full circle, it has created a circle that you could almost imagine hanging in space, like the world. The leg may move out and create bigger and bigger circles, but each will be perfectly concentric. Why? Because this moving, roving, exploring leg is firmly anchored to a fixed reference point.

This child has a consistent father.

This child's attention might not appear to be focused on the father at all. After all, he's out there drawing and exploring. But he is also firmly attached to his dad, and he takes his cues from him about how to move through the world.

The third component is the piece of paper. At the beginning it's white and blank and undefined. It is unexplored territory, and like a vast stretch of Arctic wasteland it may seem intimidating. But a father and child who form a compasslike team can cut expertly around the page. Your child will do his job. He can't help it; he has to explore. But will you do your job? Will *you* be consistent?

What if the fixed compass leg suddenly decided to move over a few inches, and then maybe up the page a fraction of an inch or two? The little leg on the other end would keep drawing but would begin to wonder why it never came around to a defined whole again. Nothing would make sense. The page would look like it had been scribbled on, with many exploratory arcs but never the satisfaction of seeing that arc curve right back around through the starting place again. The child would reach a point

77

where he'd stop exploring altogether for fear that he would suddenly find himself falling off the edge of the page.

A consistent father is a reference point that provides security, direction, and confidence in a child's life.

Conquering the World with Dad

Consistent mothers are also important. I know of one girl whose mother had numerous affairs. The mother would come back after each one and confess them to her young daughter. By now this girl has a rattled look about her. If you walk up behind her, even slowly and calmly, she's apt to turn, flinch violently, and let out a gasp. She never got used to the loud noises from her mother.

But consistent fathers have a unique importance: one of their specific roles as a father is to introduce their children to the world. We say, "It's a man's world." This does not have to mean that men chauvinistically control all the power in the world. It could mean that the world is the arena where men operate. What has been a child's traditional model of "going out into the world"? Traditionally, it has been the father.

Each morning, Dad goes through special preparations: showering, shaving, checking his briefcase, grabbing his lunch. He puts on a special uniform: suit and tie, overalls, or official dress. He gets in the car and he *goes*. He goes into the unknown, to some strange world called "work" or "the office."

Erma Bombeck tells how as a little girl, she used to play house with her dolls. She always knew what to do with the mother doll and the kid dolls, but the daddy doll was a puzzler. So, she used to dress him up and have him announce, "I'm off to work now," and she'd toss the daddy doll under the bed for the rest of the day.[1] A child's model for going off into the unknown world is often the father. He or she looks to Dad to see how exploration of the world is done.

Gordon Dalbey, author of *Healing the Masculine Soul*, argues that it is more than just a matter of male itinerary. The

The Demonstrations of Consistency

How does a man become a more consistent person and thus a more effective father? One way is for him to understand all the different ways in which his children need him to demonstrate consistency. Let me list them again. The research shows that an effective father is consistent in his:

- mood swings
- presence in the family
- keeping of promises
- morality and ethics
- daily schedule
- hobbies and interests

father is the one who calls his son and daughter out of the safe confines of the home and into the risks that are in the world. What makes children able to venture out, though, is that the risks are controlled: the father is out there for them and he is consistent. In his seminars, Dalbey uses the example of a dad who sees his kids staring out the window. It's Saturday and it's raining outside. But the dad announces, "Come on, kids, let's go outside for a walk." The mother overhears this and says, "What?! Are you crazy? They'll get wet." Now the mother isn't being a spoilsport: she's simply fulfilling her role. On a rainy day, it can be immensely pleasurable to stay inside beside a warm fire, eating popcorn. But it's also thrilling to be outside and have the rain run down your face and jump in the mud puddles and rescue worms off the sidewalk. The father tells his wife, "Don't worry. We'll put on our raincoats, and I'll make sure we come in before we get cold." It's a risky world out there, but the father is also out there and his children know he can be trusted.[2]

One of our directors at the Center comes from a family of adventurous kids. His older sister is a missionary in a Muslim country. His younger brother has taken sky-diving lessons.

79

Lowell himself has climbed mountains in the Rockies and the Himalayas. I once asked Lowell to recall for me an image of his dad. The image that immediately popped into his mind was of a pier in Lake Superior on the coast of Michigan's Upper Peninsula. "Dad would be out in the lake about five feet off the edge of the pier in water over our heads. Laurel and I would run down the pier and then leap into the water. We'd sink below the surface but then feel his hands pulling us up. He'd keep ahold of us until we splashed over to where we could stand up ourselves. Then we'd get up on the pier and do it all over again."

The water of Lake Superior is icy cold, but if you know your father will consistently be there to catch you, it's no big trick to step off that pier, or later, into a marriage and a career. Consistent fathers are important because they in particular affect the way a child views the world. Remember, if you aren't where you are supposed to be, your kids could drown.

Reference Points

When I was a child, like many kids I played baseball. My father consistently practiced with me beyond what the team did. I remember getting up on Saturday morning and hitting baseballs till I was sick of it. I'm sure, since he was the coach, he wanted me to do well. And I did, generally.

I never thought about my father's work with me until one particular year when a young boy named Tommy joined the team. Tommy was an overweight kid—uncoordinated, insecure, and destined to become the team embarrassment.

One night, after a couple weeks of watching Tommy jump out of the batter's box and swing at wild pitches and walk dejectedly out to left field, my dad suggested that Tommy stay after practice. During that evening, he pitched Tommy ball after ball until the boy finally hit one. It dribbled back out to the pitcher's mound, but Tommy and my dad were pleased.

Tommy would jump out of the batter's box when the ball was thrown for fear of getting hit. During the ball games, his jumping behavior was ridiculed by the entire team. But that evening my father showed him how to keep his elbow up; in case there was a wild pitch, he would be OK.

As the season progressed, Tommy gained more confidence. His grandparents brought him each week as he became involved in the team. Finally, toward the end of the season, we had an important game and one of those melodramatic moments where . . . you guessed it, runners were on base in a late inning and Tommy came to bat. My dad was a coach who was of the opinion that all the team members should get to bat and play during the game. (This was before the all-inclusion rule common in Little League today.) When Tommy stepped up to the plate, we all groaned. Sure, he'd had plenty of practice, but another strikeout still seemed inevitable.

Tommy left the dugout with an announcement. "I'm going to hit that ball," he said. We didn't think anything of it. It was another helpful hint my father had taught Tommy: "Tell yourself, 'I'm going to hit that ball.'" But to our surprise, he kept saying it over and over again. Not just to himself, but louder and louder so that everyone could hear. The umpire heard. The pitcher heard. My father heard. Tommy's grandparents heard.

I remember the pitcher of the opposing team smiling as Tommy swung wildly and missed the first pitch. Then came the second pitch and another wild swing. Strike two.

Tommy was alone at the plate, but not really alone. He was facing the uncertain world of the third pitch. He might be hit by it. He might be embarrassed by it. But he was also firmly anchored in an atmosphere of consistency. He had the consistent support of his grandparents, sitting faithfully in the stands. He had the regularly given guidance of his coach, my father. He believed in a consistently rehearsed vision: "I'm going to hit that ball."

The third pitch came in but looped right back out, over the second baseman's head and into right field. Tommy had hit the ball. Everybody—including Tommy—was shocked at what had happened. But not my dad. He screamed at Tommy to run to first base.

A run scored.

Unfortunately, there are also many examples of fathers' inconsistency. I know a man named Lewis who used to have a poodle named Petey. Petey would quietly sleep against the wall, and Lewis would silently sneak up to him. Suddenly, Lewis would raise his hand in the air, make claws out of his fingers, and yell, "Petey! Cat! Cat!" Petey would jump out of his sleep with a yelp and then run to the door, where he would shake and whimper.

Lewis's treatment of Petey was emblematic of what he did to his kids—the unexpected, erratic behavior that left them frightened and unsure. He undercut his kids to the point of devastation. I remember distinctly one time being in his house and hearing him cry out from another room: "Help! Help!" As I rushed into the room, I discovered him lying flat on his back on the floor. One of his adult sons was sitting on top of him, pounding the old man with his fists.

With a little composure and a lot of hesitation, I pulled the men apart. I proceeded to tell both father and son that their behavior was an embarrassment. Little did I realize that between Matt and Lewis a generational fuse had just blown. The overload had been mounting for quite some time. When Matt was just a boy, Lewis had been at one moment the wise, nurturing father, and at the next someone who verbally mocked his kids and left them to fend for themselves.

The straw that broke the camel's back was something that Matt had seen his father do the previous evening. Matt had been heading home, driving through the streets of St. Louis, when he spotted his father with a prostitute. Matt was an adult, but even so, he did not have the capacity (none of us do) to reconcile in his mind a man who can stand at the dinner table and say tearful prayers of devotion to God and the next moment be whispering his devotion to a prostitute. Matt's entire map of what the world should look like had just been scrambled.

Lewis was inconsistent in other matters. His unkept promises were devastating. He owned a building firm in St. Louis. When he was ready to retire, he told his sons that he wanted to sell them ownership of the company. One boy left a well-paying job in Michigan. Another son packed up his family in Atlanta. Not long after they moved back to Missouri, Lewis announced that he had sold the promised ownership to some other company members instead.

I know Lewis's kids. Even as adults, those who haven't sought healing are like kites floating in the sky, tethered to nothing on earth.

As part of a prison program in Minnesota, the National Center asked some of the inmates to write up an imaginary want ad where they advertised for a dad. The qualification most commonly listed by these incarcerated men was dependability. They wanted someone they could count on. One man wrote a letter to his dad that concluded, "The last time I talked to you, you said that you are gonna leave my stepmother and her kids when they grow up. Why couldn't you've waited until *we* grew up!" In essence, this inmate was wishing that if his dad had to be inconsistent, couldn't he at least have been consistently inconsistent? When it comes to reference points, kids will grasp at anything.

Ways to Improve Consistency

How does a man become a more consistent person and thus a more effective father? One way is for him to understand all the different ways in which his children need him to demonstrate consistency. Let me list them again. The research shows that an effective father is consistent:

- in his mood swings
- in his presence in the family
- in his keeping of promises
- in his morality and ethics
- in his daily schedule
- in his hobbies and interests

83

Of these categories, becoming consistent in your mood swings may prove to be the biggest struggle. But it is a struggle in which you can find victory. Many times, men who are inconsistent in their emotions are that way because they had fathers who were inconsistent. We could say that they have not been able to order their emotional lives, even as adults, because they've lacked a good reference point from which to draw a workable map of the emotional world.

"When I approached my dad, I never knew whether he was going to hug me or belt me." The place where I have heard this statement the most is among such groups as Adult Children of Alcoholics and Adult Children of Dysfunctional Families. Those who work with such groups will tell you that there are some things that all dysfunctional families have in common. One common characteristic is that the members of those families don't know what is normal. You will actually hear some children later confess that they simply assumed that all fathers drink or that all fathers are emotionally distant. What is normal? Are my dad's sudden outbursts of anger typical to most fathers? Is that quick switch from affection to impatience a common time lag? *Children of inconsistent fathers don't know.*

Another characteristic of dysfunctional families is that they don't feel. There is so much pain in a dysfunctional home that most members retreat. They think, *If I don't let myself feel anything, I won't hurt so much.* They try to become numb, but rarely do they succeed. Our emotions are part of who we are as persons. We can no more turn off our emotions than we can stop our thinking or cut off our decision making. What we can do, however, and what is done by many children in dysfunctional homes, is to ignore our emotions and not allow ourselves to express them. When we relinquish monitoring our feelings and controlling their expression, our emotions have free rein. They swing and shift about erratically and come bursting out at the time of their own choosing.

All homes have some degree of dysfunction, just as all fathers, even the effective ones, have some degree of inconsistency. If you have particular trouble governing your mood swings as a father, it may be because you too had an inconsistent dad, or a dad who was a consistently wobbly emotional reference point. But, for such men, *there is good news.*

What do you do as a mapmaker if your reference point is faulty? The answer seems logical: find a new reference point. Let someone else teach you about emotions and masculinity and fathering and living humbly with God.

The people on my staff at the National Center for Fathering often hear me refer to *mid-course corrections.* It is a nautical term that has become one of my favorites, despite the fact that, except for a stint in Vancouver, I've led a landlocked life. One of the reasons I like the term is that it is a positive way to view life crises. If we fathers can make regular and wise mid-course corrections, we can avert many life crises.

Sailors make mid-course corrections. They are sailing toward their destination, perhaps toward Vancouver, and at regular intervals the navigator takes his sextant and gets a reading on the North Star. He consults his charts. Perhaps he'll inform the captain, "We need to correct our course two degrees north-northeast."

The essence of a mid-course correction is referring to the standard, back to the reference point. For men who have had consistent fathers, this is easily done. The maps their dads have helped them sketch out are accurate, and they need only follow them faithfully. For fathers who had inconsistent dads, the mid-course correction may be a more major event. They may have to look at their emotional map, admit that it's all screwed up, and throw it overboard. Like a captain to his crew, the committed father then turns to his family—those he is responsible for bringing safely to port—and says, "Because I love you and want to guide you safely, I'm going to make the effort to draw a new map."

Find a new standard.

I've been doing research on fathers for more than five years now, and I don't think I've discovered a more profound truth than this: Strong fathers have relationships with other fathers. I'm tempted to use part of the National Center budget to buy billboard space across the country to proclaim that message in bold letters. (If you are ever at a Chinese restaurant and you find that statement inside a fortune cookie, you'll know I've had other entrepreneurial ideas.)

Strong fathers have relationships with other fathers.

For many men, that other father is their own dad—a supportive leader who modeled love and integrity. But strong fathers—many of whom have had to overcome difficult childhoods themselves—also find wisdom, encouragement, and accountability in men besides their own father. If you are looking for another fathering reference point, turn to other dads. Seek out men who are committed to their fathering, who are effective with their kids, and learn from these men. Tell them your own fathering struggles. You don't need to be embarrassed by these struggles; in fact, you will find out how common those struggles are. The difference is that effective fathers know how to respond to those struggles and will be glad to give you the inside track.

Most of all, a group of other fathers will give you encouragement. They will tell you to stick with it, and you will find strength in their friendship, which will allow you to do amazing things.

We all know that male friendships can be hard to develop. But we can use to our advantage something else we know about male friendships: they tend to develop around tasks and activities. Men will get together for a week at hunting camp. Your buddy will come over and help you work on your car. Fathering is a task that men can congregate around. In fact, they already are. There is a fathering movement afoot in this country, and the biggest evidence of it is the number of small groups being formed by men in churches and communities. These men are committed to helping each other become better fathers. (If you would like to form a fathering small group in your church or company or community, write us at the National Center. We can supply a curriculum.)

But strong fathers don't stop at relationships just with other men; our research also shows us that many of them have a relationship with God. If you are looking for an immovable standard by which to order your life, what better choice for a reference point than the "Father of the heavenly lights, who does not change like shifting shadows"? (James 1:17).

In fact, it is even a sign of an effective father that he leads his child to a point where he can say: "I've done my best to lead a consistent life before you, to be a reliable reference whereby you can find your place in the world. But, as you know, there are things I don't know and mistakes that I make. I do my best, but if you choose me as the center of your universe, you will eventually find yourself lost. Let me fulfill my most important duty as a reference point by introducing you to a more stable, more reliable reference. I have been your earthly father, but now I want you to accept a heavenly Father and map out your life according to him."

In the Middle Ages, men thought that the earth was the center of the universe and that all heavenly spheres revolved around it. This knowledge was sufficient to explain the moon's revolutions, and it also interested men in the study of the sun, which warms and feeds the earth. But then Galileo studied the sun and concluded that *it* was actually the center of the solar system and that all planets, including the earth, made their revolutions around *it*. Some redrawing of the mental maps had to take place, but then it all made sense. The universe became a much more vast and awesome place, and our maps were more useful. For instance, we could finally map time and produce accurate calendars.

The difficulty we often have in accepting God as our reference point in life stems from the fact that many of us had negative fathering models. We understandably tend to graft our relationship with our earthly father onto our relationship with our heavenly Father. A friend of mine tells me of a theology class he took years ago in seminary, in which on the first day of the semester the professor handed out a personal questionnaire. Many of the questions on the survey had to do with the student's perceptions of his father and the relationship he had with him. The surveys were collected and no more was said of them. The students forgot all about them during the rigorous months of studying the first person of the Trinity—his attributes, his work, and his words. At the end of the course, the professor handed out a second survey. This time, the students were supposed to honestly record their perceptions of God and feelings about their relationship with him. The questions, in fact, were the same as on the first survey they took, but redirected toward God the Father, not their earthly fathers. When the professor returned both sets of surveys, including the previously forgotten one, the students were astounded to find that even after a whole semester of studying about God, they still had trouble differentiating him relationally from their earthly dads. Their image of their fathers influenced their image of God.

Here's the trick. We need to understand that when God reveals himself as Father, he is not simply using "father" as a metaphor. It is not that he is *like* a father. He *is* a father, and he is *your* father. In a deep and very real sense, God *is* a father. In fact, notice in the Scriptures that when God does relate himself to earthly fathers, it is to show how much beyond comparison he is. For example, when Jesus says, "If you, then, though you are evil, know how to give good gifts to your children, *how much more* will your Father in heaven give good gifts to those who ask him!" (Matt. 7:11, emphasis added).

God is a father, and he is your father.

The benefit of this truth—the way it sets us free—is that we can let God reveal to us what type of father he is. We don't have to assume that he is an inconsistent, distant, authoritarian figure. We can let him show us who he is: compassionate, consistent, inclined to our good. I have encouraged many men to pray this prayer: "Heavenly Father, show me what type of father *you* are." God will answer this prayer. And your map will never be the same again.

Relationships with other fathers and the heavenly Father will give you the encouragement and resources you need to become more consistent in your emotional life. Yet, the process will still require some hard work. You will need to take an inventory of the emotions that well up within you, and identify the ones that cause you particular trouble as a father. You will also need to become vulnerable before your wife and kids, and verbally confess that anger or depression or some other emotion is something you struggle with, but that you are working at becoming less erratic in your mood swings. Amazingly, even this confession will add to your consistency. Your kids will see that even if your moods remain for the moment inconsistent, you at least have a consistent desire to work on them.

However, inconsistency can show up in more areas than just your emotions. Let me offer some additional tips to becoming a more consistent dad:

Keep your promises. As simple as that. In the Talmud it says, "Never promise something to a child and not give it to him, because in that way he learns to lie."[3] One of my biggest problems with promises is forgetting them. My intentions are good, but my memory is weak. So every once in a while I try to sit down and run through the list of my five kids, asking myself: Have I made any promises to any of them that I have failed to keep? I ask my wife and even the kids themselves the same question.

Granted, there are times when a promise is impossible to keep. Circumstances can get out of our control. During such times, it's important that you explain fully why you can't do what you said you were going to do. Be careful not to pass quickly over the promise with a quick "Forget about it" or "These things happen, OK?" or "I'll make it up to you later." Remember, the obligation is still yours. You assumed it when you gave your word. You need to demonstrate that you consider your promise to be a valid and binding thing; if you can't fulfill it, you are at least going to make the effort to provide a satisfying explanation.

Guard your word. If you begin to find yourself making more explanations than you do fulfillments of promises, you should ask yourself if you're promising too much. Be wise. If conditions look favorable for a trip to the zoo on Saturday, but you know of

89

other obligations that might make the trip unlikely, be careful about waltzing into the living room and announcing, "Hey, kids, whaddaya say we go see the elephants this weekend?" The only elephants you see may be the ones tromping through the house Saturday morning disappointedly trumpeting, "But you promised. But you promised." Your word is your bond.

Standardize your work schedule. If at all possible, leave for work at the same time each morning, and come home from work at the same time each night. Such a schedule adds to the atmosphere of regularity and predictability in your home.

If your business requires that you do a lot of traveling, consider typing up an itinerary for your wife to share with the kids. That way, she can keep your kids informed about where their dad is at all times. Daddy's not "gone." He's in Chicago, or boarding a plane right now to go to Atlanta, or in a meeting for the next hour at the Hyatt Regency in Kansas City.

Plan regularly scheduled family time. When you sit down with your pocket calendar to plan out your week or your month, plan the week or month with your children in mind. Write in (no "penciling in") evenings and hours throughout the period that are designated family times. Then, as with any other priority appointment (if indeed your children and consistent fathering are priorities), protect those times. A colleague of mine, Blake Ashdown, who is the president of a busy resort company in Michigan, was recently quoted in the *Wall Street Journal* as saying that when it came to balancing work and family activities, "I've begun to control the activities in my life rather than their controlling me."[4] Believe it or not, you *can* schedule your other activities around your family, rather than giving something else your prime time and squeezing in your kids during what's left over. The key, though, is scheduling. You have to plan ahead; otherwise, something important will always seem to pop up and take you away from home.

Plan regular family time, and notify your family: "Every Friday night, I'm planning on simply being yours."

Develop a hobby, trade, or skill that you and your family

enjoy doing. It should be an activity that you all come back to time and time again. It can be something as consuming as a family business ("Smith & Sons Body Shop") or as enjoyable as a hobby (gardening or canoeing). I just met a pilot who has taught all five of his daughters to fly. Some families backpack. Others milk cows. Last Christmas, one of our staff members saw a group of carolers in the mall. He recognized some of the faces and thought it must be a group from a church here in town, until Bob Taussig walked up to him with a video camera. "See these?" Bob said, motioning with his camera to the choir. "They're all mine." Doctor Bob was the father, father-in-law, and grandfather of a group of forty-three. He had signed them up to sing in the mall.

This shared activity will provide some good time to spend together as a family, but it will also enhance your fathering consistency by giving your children something by which they can define their family. They know who their family is: "We're the ones who gather around the piano and sing" or "We're the ones who raise Labrador retrievers." In the old days, these shared family activities were crucial in establishing stable family structures. Families were known by their activities (or occupations), and many of our ancestors even derived their names from them: Baker, Fuller, Miller.

These family activities can also be a wonderful boon for you. If you had a tough childhood, this can be a way of reliving it in a more positive way. If you were always interested in toy trains as a kid but never owned any, here's your chance to buy some now—for the kids, of course.

Avoid the trap of trying to make up for lost time. I don't know what your situation is. Maybe you're disappointed about how you've fathered up to this point. Maybe you are divorced and living away from your kids. Whatever your situation, avoid the urge to try to make up for lost time. Don't throw wild extravaganzas for your child simply because you haven't expressed your love enough in the past. Whenever I go to a Kansas City Royals baseball game, I can't help noticing the kids in the sta-

91

dium who have been loaded down with enough baseball paraphernalia that they could open their own stand in the parking lot. The fathers of those kids are overcompensating for lost time. The kid can't decide whether to wave his pennant, his inflatable baseball bat, or his giant foam "We're #1" hand. Not a vendor goes by without the father signaling, grabbing for his wallet, and buying the child peanuts, popcorn, Cokes, hot dogs.

When it comes to consistency, you need to realize that these "blowouts" are part of a pendulum swing. A month of not hearing from their father and then *pow*. Two weeks of scarcely seeing Dad around the house and then *pow*. It can really shake a kid up.

It's possible to be consistent with your children even when they don't live with you. You are only a phone call or a letter away from being a regular, consistent part of your child's life. Children need regular and predictable contact with their fathers. If you are away from your kids, a phone call once a week is more beneficial to their development than four trips to Disney World strewn haphazardly throughout the year.

Effective fathers are consistent fathers. When our little mapmakers head out into the world, they need a firm feel for where home is, and they need to feel that they know what they'll find when they get there.

Six

SECRET 4: Protecting and Providing

The fourth secret of effective fathers is that they strongly accept their role as protector and provider for their families.

Last week, a missionary and his family stayed in our home. They are missionaries in Ontario, Canada, and work among the Native Americans there. Lately this man has begun traveling to reservations across North America working on establishing fathering programs for Native American men. He's responding to the crisis of Indian masculinity.

He told me that the tribe he lives with in Ontario is a matriarchal society, but that this is a relatively recent phenomenon. The men had been the leaders of that culture as recently as a hundred years ago. They fulfilled their role as protectors by going to war against hostile neighbors. They fulfilled their role as providers by hunting wild game and fishing the lakes. We all know how development has shrunk the hunting grounds since that time. Hunting is no longer a viable means of supporting a tribe. We also know how the government has established reservations and moved the Indians onto them. The tribal wars are gone. So are the elk and buffalo. So are the traditional expressions of male roles.

When the Native American men finally resigned themselves and came to the reservation, they found the women doing what the women had always traditionally done, but now circumstances were different. In the past, the men had gone off hunting and fighting, while the women had remained at home, tending the livestock and tilling the ground. Under the new system, the women's activities did not change, but their significance did. Today, on these Ontario reservations, women own the sheep and have deeds to the land. When a man marries, his bride does not join him and his family; he instead leaves his family to join hers.

Now I'm not going to argue whether a matriarchal society is better or worse than a patriarchal one. But I *am* going to argue that when a father relinquishes the role of protector and provider, something very important is lost. The Native American male culture is in crisis. My missionary friend can quote you the latest rates of alcoholism, drug abuse, and violent crime found on the reservations.

In North American culture at large, the father's role as protector against danger and financial provider has not disappeared to the degree that it has on the reservation, but it has become less visible. This may seem strange to say, since a common complaint about fathers is that they only contribute to the family in one way: a paycheck. What I'm talking about is visibility—what we fathers hold as important and what our children *perceive* about our priorities.

My home state of Kansas is steeped in pioneer lore. We grew up hearing stories of covered wagons and sod houses. For pioneer children, a father's protection and provision was close to the surface. They saw their father's rifle handy and maybe even saw him use it against horse thieves, hostile Indians, wolves, or rattlesnakes. They saw their father out in the pens, slaughtering a hog, and hanging it in the smokehouse. When they sat down at the dinner table, they knew his hand had provided the meal, including the corn muffins they ate, made from the corn their father harvested and hauled to the mill for grinding.

PROTECTING AND PROVIDING

Effective fathers had significantly higher scores in these two basic fathering roles:

Protecting: When a crisis occurs, fathers take a leadership role in dealing with it calmly, effectively, and constructively, and in restoring stability in the family.

Providing: Fathers instill security by having a steady, reliable income and providing for the material needs of the family.

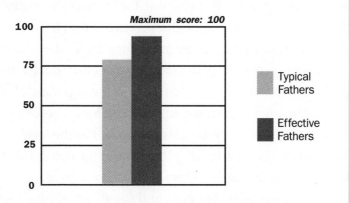

Maximum score: 100

Typical Fathers

Effective Fathers

Effective fathers scored 93% of the maximum score in protecting and providing for their children. Typical fathers scored 82% of the maximum score. Historically, fathers have understood and placed a high priority on providing for and protecting their children. Of the seven secrets, this scale was the closest in comparison, yet still significantly different.

Things are similar today, but not exactly the same. A father regularly protects his children by paying local taxes to support a police force and federal taxes to support a military. But his kids don't see him doing these important things, just like they don't see him paying their health insurance premiums or having the mechanic check the brake lines on the car. A father still provides for his family by putting in his hours and bringing home a paycheck. But a paycheck is just a slip of paper, while a dressed-out hog hanging in the smokehouse is much more tangible. With direct deposit services, a father's wages can be just a blip on a teller's computer screen.

In the old days, a child could see his father outside splitting the firewood and hauling it inside to fuel the stove. The child knew his warmth was directly dependent on his dad's hard work. Now, the fuel flows into our stoves invisibly from pipes laid underground. Even in the cities, times are different. In the novel *How Green Was My Valley,* set at the turn of the century, the Morgan boys all join their father to work in the coal mines. Each Friday, the mines pay out wages and the men collect their coins and currency. The wives and mothers meet their husbands at the door with the tin canister that stays in the cupboard above the stove. The men drop the coins into the box, where they clang against the side. The little kids peer into it as the level of provision grows. They ask to carry the canister back to the kitchen. It is a weighty thing their fathers have accomplished.[1]

The pioneer days are gone and should not return. But what we must be careful not to let go of is the importance that we fathers place on our roles as protectors and providers. Our children need us to protect and provide for them, *and they need to see us doing it.* In research with effective fathers, one of their common characteristics is that they take protection and provision strongly to heart. This aspect of protection and provision is the fourth secret of effective fathers.

Responding in Time of Crisis

While some protective issues may be less visible than in days when we circled the wagons, there are still plenty of occasions where a father is called to rise up and protect those he loves. These can be major crises like a father's unemployment, a wife's sickness, or a child's drug habit. They can be minor crises like a scraped knee, a lost pet, or a broken washer or dryer. Some major crises can be so complex and so painful that you'd almost rather be back in the 1800s wrestling a grizzly bear instead.

Being able to respond to crises isn't easy. It takes fortitude and commitment. It takes more fortitude than I thought I had when I saw my son Micah there in the hospital bed, restlessly turning from side to side. Micah moaned as I helped him with the urinal every hour, moaned as I tried to reassure him that I was there, that he was going to be OK. It wasn't a sound a four-year-old should be making. I watched the outline of his right foot fidgeting under the blanket. His left foot was still, the lower part of his leg braced and heavily wrapped for the two fractures he had suffered.

Crossing the street seemed so simple, but for Micah it was an adventure. He'd always been cautious and obedient; he'd never even left the yard on his own. I can only guess what could have been going through his mind. When I think about it now, I have to conclude that an angel was out there sitting next to him, maybe on a matching three-wheeler, a riding buddy for the afternoon. When Micah rolled up to the edge of the driveway, this angel could have whispered something to him, or caused a tree to wave in the wind—anything to delay his five-foot venture for a second or two and keep him from meeting the bumper of the silver Honda face to face. He caught the back tire instead.

At first, the driver thought she'd run over a branch, and she continued to the end of the block before she looked in her rearview mirror. Then she saw my child lying on his side, twisted around the plastic tricycle. She frantically came back to join his mother, sister, and brother, who had responded to his groans.

I was in the basement, working on a broken storm window. I can even remember thinking, *I wonder what Micah's doing out in the front yard?* but I was too involved and didn't respond to the impulse. Kids will be kids, after all. You can't protect them from everything. Some people learn better by going through something on their own, right?

I still don't have it all worked out.

Upon arriving at the hospital, we learned that the best orthopedic doctor in town just happened to be there already, tending a patient in the next room. We were assured that Micah would come through fine. In fact, he has. The only evidence of his accident is his constant retelling of it to anyone who will listen.

I hope Micah has learned the lesson not to ride in the street, but I think the greatest lessons of the incident have been reserved for me, his father. I learned how dangerous this world can be for those I love. I hesitated to put Micah's story in this book, because I know I am writing to some fathers who haven't been as fortunate as I. I know that some of you visit grave sites where you silently calculate the dates on the granite marker and wonder why the sweet life of your child had to be so short. I know that some of you have different kinds of pain: broken relationships with your wife or children; a child's drinking problems, teenage pregnancy or school expulsion; financial predicaments. Micah didn't die, but a lot of my frivolity in fathering did. I soberly realized that *crises will happen in my family.* I need to be prepared to respond to them.

I also learned that I don't have all the answers. On the front end, I can't be all places at all times. There may be some crises I can prevent, but I can't protect my family from all that will occur before it occurs. On the back end, I can't explain to my family why these crises have to happen. I couldn't tell my wife, Dee, when she asked me, why Micah wasn't as obedient this time as he'd always been in the past.

The only thing a father does have control over is his response in the face of crisis. It lies within each one of us to rise to the occasion and do what needs to be done. You stride out the front doors of your home, take a quick moment to size up the situation in the street, calmly give your oldest daughter all the information she needs to call the ambulance, and then kneel by your son's side, brush his hair out of his eyes, and tell him, "It's going to be all right. Daddy's here."

A father's positive response in a time of crisis is crucial. While

Safety Checklist

A protecting father does some of his best work before a crisis occurs. You can help prevent certain crises by making sure that your children are educated about certain safety precautions and emergency responses. Use the following as a checklist:

☐ My children know the proper way to exit our house in case of a fire.

☐ My children know when and how to call 911.

☐ My children know what things in the house (matches, poisons, power tools, etc.) are off-limits to them.

☐ My children know how to respond in the event of a tornado or earthquake.

☐ My children know how to respond if caught outside in a lightning storm.

☐ My children are aware of the dangers of drug use, and have been taught how to say no to dealers and peer pressure.

☐ My kids have been taught that premarital abstinence is the safest means to avoid contracting AIDS.

☐ My children have been warned about playing or riding their bikes heedlessly in the streets.

☐ My older children have been trained in CPR.

☐ My children, for their own safety as much as for their pleasure, have been taught how to swim.

☐ All my children, including my three-year-old, have memorized their phone number and street address in case they get lost.

a father might not be able to prevent a crisis, his actions can do a lot to determine the outcome when the crisis does occur. Learn grace under fire. Handle these times with a level head and execute the positive actions that need to be taken to restore the family's normal operation. Some crises may seem paralyzing, but in every case there are always actions you can take which, even if they don't (or can't) resolve the crisis, will at least buffer your family against greater damage. Take action.

"What I Saw My Father Do"

A father's positive response is also crucial in an indirect way. One day—and it won't take long for that day to come—your children will know the same thing you know: crises happen. In some moment of danger, they will be called to respond in such a way as to spell the difference for themselves between life and loss. In that crucial moment, their minds will scan backward for knowledge of how to react. In particular, they will be looking for models who have responded to crises. Specifically, they will be remembering you, their father.

Ruth Calkin is a poet. Apparently, a newspaper article taught her something about the modeling power of a father. She wrote this poem:

> Just this week
> I read a newspaper account
> Of a thirteen-year-old boy
> Who saved his brother's life
> By driving him to a hospital
> In his father's car.
> Never having driven before
> His explanation was simple:
> "I just did what I saw my father do."[2]

I just did what I saw my father do. In some ways that statement is repeated after every crisis, even if it is never verbalized.

"Why did you so quickly get your own child the medical attention she needed?"

I just did what I saw my father do.

"Why did you stick it out with your son in rehab?"

I just did what I saw my father do.

"Why did you get mad and throw that wrench at the washing machine?"

I just did what I saw my father do.

"Why did you turn and run?"

I just did what I saw my father do.

It works both ways. A father must model the type of grace under pressure that he wants his son or daughter to emulate. If we avoid coming apart during a crisis and instead take positive action, we not only help our children survive this immediate crisis, but help prepare them for future ones. Our protection as a father can extend even beyond our presence.

There are six things effective fathers do that help make them better protectors of their children:

1. Adopt a healthy attitude toward crises. First, effective fathers recognize that crises will occur and therefore are not caught totally off guard when they do. Second, they accept beforehand that one of their roles as father is to be a protector of the family. Consequently, they are ready to step forward and take action when necessary. Third, they also believe that a family can actually gain more strength from a resolved crisis than the harm that has been suffered.

The Chinese character that translates into English as *crisis* is a combination of two characters: one that means *dangerous* and another that means *opportunity.* A crisis can be a dangerous opportunity. It can be a healthy, providentially designed way to test and refine your own beliefs and practices, or it can cause the very ground you walk on to crumble beneath you.

Glen Elder wrote a book entitled *Children of the Great Depression.* In particular he was looking for the different ways that families were affected by the Depression of the 1930s, a crisis of large magnitude that was not controllable. Elder found that adolescents from economically deprived homes came out of the Depression more capable of handling other crises than the adolescents whose families were largely unaffected by the Depression. As he states:

> *However onerous the task may be, there is gratification and even personal growth to be gained in being chal-*

103

lenged by a real undertaking if it is not excessive or exploitative.[3]

2. Identify the role models from whom you learned how to deal with crises. If necessary, choose a new one. When we are in a crisis, we go through a quick déjà vu experience. We think back to similar experiences from our childhood to try to establish some reference points and make comparisons to the present crisis. Those of us whose fathers handled crises effectively have a wealth of memories to draw from, but the rest of us have to rely upon our friendships with other men, both as children and now as adults. If your role model for handling crises is a negative one, then choose a more fruitful model. But choose one now, before a crisis occurs, and start your research. That way, when something does happen, you will be prepared to immediately ask the question, How would Uncle Dave handle this? or, What would my friend Joe do?

Your male friendships will also be instructional. If fathers are going to deal effectively with crises, we need to be in touch with people who are going through hard times and learn to empathize with their situations. This will give us the opportunity to think about how we would respond and plan the best way to reach out to those in need. If we can objectively think through a disaster that affects others, we can begin to develop plans for responding positively when a crisis strikes closer to home.

3. Regain your confidence after a crisis by enjoying the support of other fathers. Being a father is tough. Fathers can gain confidence about their plans and decisions through the support of other fathers. There is a great feeling of camaraderie in interacting with other dads, hearing that you aren't the only one who struggles, learning from their successes and failures, encouraging them and being encouraged in your fathering.

No one is born with fully developed fathering skills, so there will be failures. The support of other fathers can enable you to gain back your confidence. This is not simply an attitude check. It's a bold effort to get back on the horse, to replace the memory of falling off with one of galloping at a breakneck pace together across the fields, the horse responding eagerly to even the slightest tug on the reins. People who exude confidence are easy to follow, and if your family is convinced that you believe it when you say, "Everything's going to be fine," then you've already released much of the tension out of the crisis. Confidence helps you to create an atmosphere of stability.

4. Understand your own foundation as a man. In our research, fathers who scored high in being able to deal with crises also scored significantly higher on their responses to male identity issues. In other words, they related the handling of crises to feeling comfortable being a man.

In 1 Corinthians 16, Paul is finishing up his letter to the church but adds one final admonition for them to rise to the occasion: "Be on your guard; stand firm in the faith; *be men of courage;* be strong" (v. 13, emphasis added). In the Old Testament there is an incident when Israel and Philistia are at war. The Israelite army has foolishly brought the ark of the covenant into battle and for the moment seems ready to overwhelm the Philistines. But God intends to use the Philistines to judge Israel's disobedience with the ark. The troops are rallied with this call: "Take courage and be men, O Philistines, lest you become slaves to the Hebrews, as they have been slaves to you; therefore, be men and fight" (1 Sam. 4:9, NASB).

Take courage and be men.

Be men and fight against the crises in your home.

In other words, take confidence in how God has created you. When crises occur, simply say, "This is it! It is for occasions just like this that I was made a father and a man."

Now the ideal man is not Rambo in the midst of battle. You reach the ideal simply by feeling comfortable, even enthusiastic about your role as a man and father. It extends confidence to your entire life-style and personality.

Are you satisfied in your roles as a male? Are you comfortable being head of the household, or do some of the responsibilities make you feel insecure? Insecurity leaves men vulnerable to crises. But fathers who are firmly grounded in their masculinity and who feel good about themselves are willing to go through a crisis, and will more likely be prepared when one does occur.

5. In times of crisis, talk with your children. Fathers who deal successfully with crises have healthy verbal interaction with their kids. They are able to talk things through, during and after a crisis. The effective father can openly communicate with his children, and his children feel they have an open channel to their dad at any time, concerning any subject.

As they were wheeling Micah into surgery, I was able to spend several minutes with him in the brightly lit hallway. "How are you feeling, Micah?" I asked.

We were able to talk through his feelings, and I found that to some degree he was looking forward to all the neat things he was going to see.

"Now listen," I told him. "Your mother and I are going to be right outside here in the waiting room. We'll be around. In fact, we'll see you before you see us. You'll be asleep for a while." I was able to reassure him that we'd be there for him when he was done, and hearing that he was handling it well really helped to calm me down, too.

Many a solution has been discovered by the attentive ears of fathers who can obtain and utilize the collective insight of their families. Daily interaction with our kids has rewards that extend far beyond the potential benefits it brings to solving crises.

6. Maintain consistent discussion with your wife, as well as with your kids. Effective fathers who have healthy interaction with their wives are familiar with the special abilities their mates have and know how to utilize those assets in a tense situation. The importance of healthy marital interaction is shown graphically during crises. Couples who have lost a child are much more likely to divorce than couples who have not faced such disaster.[4] One of the reasons for this is that no one grieves in the same way and at the same rate. For wives, the grief is immediate and intense. Men are more likely to put off the grieving for the moment, to say, "Well, let's get on with our lives." But men will revisit that grief later, and it will be just as painful and intense.

The danger is that the husband will consider the wife to be helplessly cowardly, while the wife will consider the husband to be callous and coldhearted. If the two are unable to communicate their differences, a downward spiral begins that could eventually end their marriage.

When a crisis occurs to parents who communicate regularly with one another, both are able to get positive results from discussion, both as a couple in private *and* with their children. Again, husbands will ideally have strong communication habits with their wives already established, and discussion will be a natural response in times of crisis.

I have a feeling that we live in a day in which crises—major crises—are going to occur. This isn't a gloom-and-doom prophecy, but a realistic look at what I see in the media and what is happening around me every day. Economic, political, health, and religious pressures will rise. Children will need support and guidance from their fathers more than ever before.

Sometimes I can still hear the sound of my son's moaning that day in the hospital bed, and it scares me, because tragedies can happen for no apparent reason, and many times there's nothing we can do to stop them. But we can do our best to model healthy virtues and prepare ourselves to stand beside our children when crises occur. And we can pray to God the Father and ask him to keep his angels hovering nearby when our children ride up to the edges of curbs.

A Roof Over Their Heads

Providing financially for your family is related to protecting them. When you provide a roof over their heads, you protect them against snow and hail and lightning storms. When you provide grocery money, you protect them against starvation. We could even say that when you pay taxes, you protect your children against crime, since a portion of those taxes goes to support a police force.

I was surprised when the numbers came up on the computer screen and revealed that financial provision is one of the seven secrets of effective fathers. I guess I half expected these effective dads to agree with the common sentiment that says, "Oh, if a man thinks his work is important, then obviously he's depriving his kids." Our culture for the past few decades has perhaps overemphasized the role of father as financial provider, but the effective father says, "While financial provision is not my *only* role, it *is* a role and one I consider important."

What effective fathers tell us is that we should not feel guilty about going to work. If we never come home from work, then we should feel guilty, but while doing our jobs and drawing our paychecks we should feel proud that we are faithfully meeting the needs of our children and dutifully fulfilling our roles as fathers.

If you question whether financial provision should be so closely linked to fathering effectiveness, let me ask you some questions: What would happen if you lost your job? How would such a loss affect your relationship with your kids? Would you feel like you were a poor father? The question is not *should* you feel like you were a poor father, but *would* you? It seems to be an issue of fathering motivation and satisfaction. In a recent study of African-American fathers, researchers found that as the economic sufficiency of these men grew, there was a corresponding increase in the active participation they had with their children.[5] Apparently, there is a certain standard that fathers need to reach in order to feel good about their fathering role.

The way in which fathers respond to economic loss also affects their relationship with their children. In a study of job and income loss, fathers who responded irritably and with pessimism to a loss (something which is certainly easy to do) were more punitive and less nurturant in their interactions with their children. The author of the study goes further to state, "These fathering behaviors increase the child's risk of socioemotional problems, deviant behavior, and reduced aspirations and expectations."[6]

Fathers may be dealing with their own version of Maslow's

Hierarchy of Needs. Remember that theory? It says that we must attend to our basic needs of food, shelter, and clothing before we have the freedom to deal with loftier needs like meaning and self-fulfillment. It may be that fathers feel the need to attend to their children's survival needs so strongly that, unless they do so adequately, they don't feel the freedom to perform other fathering duties such as showing affection or spiritual equipping. In fact, one characteristic that emerged from the data on effective fathers is that they closely link their role of financial provider to their other fathering roles. For example, at the same time as they are financially providing, they are also being a *modeler* of consistency and the work ethic. They link provision to issues of leadership in the home and dealing with crises.

Financial provision is important.

I suspect that most of you reading this book are already holding down a job or are actively seeking one. You wouldn't be satisfied if the only advice effective fathers had to give you on financial provision was: "Get a job." But there is another dimension to the provider role in which effective fathers differ from all other dads.

But first I should probably tell you what effective fathers are *not* saying. They are not saying that making more money leads to greater fathering satisfaction. Almost all of the men identified as effective fathers were in the middle-income bracket. The level of income is not as important as a *steady* income that provides for the *basic* needs of the family. Effective fathers are also not saying that they need to be the sole provider for their family. (However, the fathers in this study whose wives worked fewer than fifteen hours per week reported significantly higher ratings of satisfaction when it came to providing for the family income.)

The added dimension that effective fathers bring to their provider role is a knowledge of their family's needs. They begin with an understanding of what it will take to support their wife and kids and what it will take to foster their children's aspirations; this understanding then governs their choice of their place in the work force.

I've talked to a number of men who have found satisifaction in their financial provider role. Many of these experiences I can combine in a composite portrait of a man I'll call Vernon.

Vernon is like most professional men in his adult timetable. He went to college for four years, interviewed with an engineering firm his senior year, and essentially started his career right after graduation. He renewed an acquaintance with a college friend named Jill. They were married for two years before they had their first child. Vernon was thus in his job for four years before they started a family. When, as a single man, he made his career choice and chose a company to work for, he had made his decision based on how he could best use his interests, talents, gifts, and opportunities.

In fewer than five years after the birth of their first child, Vernon and Jill added two more children to their family, and Vernon received three more job promotions. But he began to feel dissatisfied. Something wasn't coming together.

"I can't figure it out," he said on one occasion. "I mean, my job doesn't require much travel and rarely do I put in overtime, but I really feel like something's being taken away from my kids. Or maybe I just feel split in two. I go to work, but when I'm there I don't feel like a father. Some days, when it's five o'clock and I head home, it strikes me that I haven't thought about my kids all day long. It makes me feel like I'm a poor excuse for a dad."

Vernon also wondered how successfully he was providing for his children. All the bills were getting paid, and some money was getting stashed away each month. Still, how do you know? When is enough enough?

What Vernon needed to do, and what he eventually did, was make a new career choice. Oh, he didn't switch occupations or leave his company; he didn't even transfer out of his position. In fact, he stayed right where he was. His new career choice was actually a new career *choosing*. He went back through the process of choosing his occupation, but in the context of his new frame of mind. The first time he had chosen, he was a single man; now, he was married with three children. In the past, his interests, talents, gifts, and opportunities were an end in them-selves (How can I best fulfill them?); now, they were only a means (How can I best *use* them to provide for my family?).

Vernon sat down and figured out what his family's financial needs were. He had three kids. Lately he and Jill had been talking about adding another child, so he figured this future baby into his thinking too. The idea apparently struck him that he could approach this as he had done so often at work. What are the grocery needs for a family of six? What is the monthly mortgage payment? How much does it cost to keep the kids in clothes? He also tried to calculate in amounts for encouraging his children's interests—things like gymnastics classes and Girl Scouts. Ver-non found he could use the family budget for most of these calculations, but now he wasn't thinking of the budget as a record of spending, but more as a set of funding goals.

Before long, Vernon had a bottom line: *To provide for my family at a level that meets their basic needs and that pleases me in terms of fulfilling a few of everyone's wants too, I need to make a certain amount this year.* He also had a good idea how his income would need to grow over the years to accommodate whatever contributions he'd want to make toward his kids' col-lege expenses. All along the line, he and Jill were making choices. Jill would work only when the youngest went off to first grade, and then only part-time. They decided that they would not buy cars for their kids but would save up for one or two extravagant family vacations before the kids left home.

With the bottom line written down before him, Vernon could decide: *What can I do that will best use my interests, talents, gifts, and opportunities for the provision of my family?* Along with an adequate salary, he needed a job that didn't keep him away from home inordinately. While Vernon was prepared to leave his pres-ent job, he found he didn't have to. He was already making above his projected need and was generally happy at his work. On Monday morning, Vernon woke up as usual, took a shower, broke up a fight at the breakfast table over cereal boxes, and kissed his wife at the door as he headed off to work. Nothing had changed but his perspective, and yet that made all the difference in the world.

When you begin with a knowledge of your family's needs and *then* make a career choice, you gain some wonderful advantages. First, you help relieve the tension caused by a perception that your work week is competing against your home life. The process Vernon went through essentially subordinated his work to his home. The decision to be at work, even at his particular job, was a decision that he made for his children and their future. He could feel good about being at work.

Also, when you know your needs and then make choices based upon them, it's easy to determine whether or not you are successfully providing for your children. You can see it on paper. In my family, my wife and I have calculated how much it costs each day to "run" our family. We revise the figure regularly. The latest revision occurred when at the dinner table one evening I found myself still hungry and reached for seconds. There weren't any. My two growing boys had wiped out the casserole. I must have looked pretty pathetic when I told my wife, "But I'm still hungry." Dee said, "You know, I can't remember the last time we had any leftovers."

When you know your family's daily financial needs, it's a nice feeling to receive your biweekly paycheck, divide it by fourteen days, and know that you've met those needs. It's the *knowing* that's nice. You don't have to wonder.

In the same way, this process can provide a standard for success in your career. Most men will tell you that they are striving for success in their occupations, but few men can tell you when they achieve it. Happiness fades in and out. Salary levels seem unsatisfying when you can always find someone making more money than you (just ask any major league baseball player!). But when your goal is providing for your family and you know your family's provision needs, you can know when you are successful in reaching your goal.

When Adam sinned, God pronounced his curse, and the curse involved men's work. God did not declare work unimportant or evil. He still called Adam to it, but he also made the process of work more toilsome: thorns and thistles and the sweat of our brows. Notice the wording of the curse, though: "Cursed is the ground because of you; through painful toil you will eat of it all the days of your life. It will produce thorns and thistles for you, and you will eat the plants of the field. By the sweat of your brow, you will eat your food. . . " (Gen. 3:17-19).

Men who approach their work as a means of fulfillment in and of itself will come face to face with the curses, toil, thorns, thistles, and sweat mentioned in these verses. But men who approach work for its results, though they still experience the toilsome effects of the curse, also experience the satisfaction of the results: You will eat. They know when they've been successful.

Finally, knowing your family's needs and choosing jobs accordingly can make career changes much less stressful. When an opportunity for a pay increase presents itself, it's amazing how urgently we devote ourselves to those extra dollars. But when you can look at your family's budget and say, "Hey, wait a second, I don't *need* to make a mint, I just need to meet my family's needs," then you have a freedom that lets you make decisions according to your own standards instead of your company's or your neighbor's. Some of the pressure is removed. When you make decisions according to a family-needs criterion, you are also inclined to consider your children's other, nonfinancial needs. For example, Will this job allow me to spend the amount of time that I want to with my kids? or, Will taking this particular job model the type of virtuous career choice that I want my child to make some day, or is there something shady about this offer? Effective fathers make sure that the workplace complements the home.

Providing in a Challenging Economy

Our nation's economy is becoming more and more complex. I've become so tired of hearing that this next generation of people will likely be the first in America's history not to exceed the economic achievements of their parents that I have given in and decided to believe it. The American Dream has always been: "You can exceed your father." If this dream needs rewriting due to economic realities, I like how effective fathers are rewriting it. They are telling their children, *"We* can exceed *our* fathers." They have translated the dream from performance first to relationship first. Committed dads are saying to their children, "We're here to help one another," and they are pulling together in a spirited camaraderie of survival similar to what was experienced in many homes during the Great Depression. They are pooling resources together for each other's good.

What distinguishes effective fathers from all other dads is that they know their children's needs and then work to meet those needs. This applies not only to the pot roast on the table for the evening meal, but also to the child's own economic future. Effective fathers know early on what their children's plans and dreams are. They provide steady affirmation of those plans and dreams as the child grows and then work to provide the necessary education to support those dreams. This education may be a university degree, a vo-tech diploma, or a stint in the armed services. An effective father's provision for his child includes providing for his child's own entrance into the economic world. When he has sufficiently done so, the father and child become a team, able to function amid the complexities of a challenging economy.

Seven

SECRET 5:
Loving Their
Mother

Through union with a woman, children are born.

Through communion with that same woman, secure and confident children are born.

Be suspicious of any book on fathering that does not include a chapter on marriage.

The fathering process is like an axe used in the forest to clear a place for a home or used to split firewood to feed stoves for warmth and comfort. An axe is judged by its usefulness—its ability to function properly. Hopefully, the handle is made of good solid wood that won't split under pressure. The lathe has formed it straight and true. The axe handle is the leverage point. When the woodsman swings the axe to accomplish his purposes, the power courses through the axe handle and into the blade.

The axe head is our focus, where the power of the axe handle finally resides. It is what we desire to be sharp and effective, out in the world faithfully doing its work, successfully cutting through massive trunks of cedar and hackberry.

If effective fathering is like a smooth-cutting axe, then there is one other component that needs to be mentioned. That is the

117

wedge that joins with the axe handle, expanding it out where the handle meets the head to keep the head from slipping. Without the wedge, it doesn't make any difference how solid and true the axe handle is. If the wedge is missing, the head will bite weakly into the trees and eventually fly off altogether. This crucial component is your wife. She expands your influence as a father, filling you out and letting you touch your children more tightly and across a wider surface. There's less chance of slippage. She also channels your power and allows you to be more effective with your children.

I can hear some old man in some backyard working on a stack of firewood, muttering, "Boy, they don't make axes like they used to." If he's thinking of our analogy, he's unfortunately right. We live in an age of divorce and halfhearted attempts at marriage. Today when we think of single-parent households, we think of divorcees and unwed mothers. But surprisingly, in the 1950s most single-parent households were composed of widows.[1] The rate of divorce in America has more than doubled since that earlier time.[2] *The effect on our children is devastating.*

The fifth secret of effective fathers—the fifth way in which they significantly differ from all other dads—is in their commitment to cultivate a strong marital relationship with their children's mother.

I have struggled with understanding this secret. It seems to leave little room for variance. What about fathers whose wives have left them? How can these men apply this secret after they have experienced marital failure? The secret creates a great difficulty for those men who sincerely love their children and want to be effective dads, but who have a hard time loving their wives.

Certainly, many people argue that the father-child relationship is one relationship and the husband-wife is another, and that the one can remain strong despite the other. Interestingly, the biggest political issue regarding fathering uses this premise. One nationally known organization is named Fathers for Equal Rights and has often argued successfully in court that fathers are important in the parenting of a child. They have won custody

MARITAL RELATIONSHIP

Fathers' marital interaction scores were obtained by surveying the following items:

- Providing children with a healthy model for masculine behavior toward women.
- Cultivating a strong marriage by scheduling time alone with their wife.
- Working toward having a romantic, sexually satisfying marriage.

The following chart will help demonstrate how strong fathers compared with other fathers.

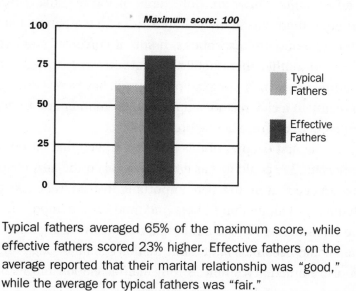

Typical fathers averaged 65% of the maximum score, while effective fathers scored 23% higher. Effective fathers on the average reported that their marital relationship was "good," while the average for typical fathers was "fair."

battles and increased access rights for divorced dads. In its January 1990 issue, *Playboy* magazine ran an article heralding the 1990s as the Decade of the Dad. While such a sweeping title might promise to promote fathering in a broad sense, the article chose to focus on the limited political aspect of courts granting divorced dads more access to their children. The marriage relationship was not considered to be part of the fathering role.

Similarly, there is much political activity swirling around homo-sexual fathers. Should gay couples be allowed to adopt children? Both issues reflect a commonly held assumption in our society: The father-child relationship exists independently of the husband-wife relationship.[3]

Despite the arguments that children in single-parent homes can succeed in the same ways children in two-parent families can, the best researchers will readily point out that children of divorce suffer significantly for it.[4] Half of the mother-only families live below the poverty line. Adolescents from mother-only families are more likely to be sexually active, susceptible to peer pressure, abusive of drugs and alcohol, and low-scoring in school exams. These are only some of the negative effects.[5] Granted, there are many children from single-parent homes who are wonderful exceptions. If you are divorced from your children's mother, there is still a lot that you can do to make your children exceptions. For example, you still have a responsibility to maintain a civil relationship with their mother and to never undercut or disgrace her before them.

In the first chapter of this book we argued that fathers are important. We could just as easily have taken the next chapter and argued that mothers are important. Instead, we'll take this chapter and argue that fathers *and* mothers are important. At the very least we have to admit that if it wasn't for a woman, no man could become a father. But we don't go far enough unless we also admit that without a strong marital relationship, no man can become a highly effective father.

I'm sorry if these statements step on some toes. I know I may be setting myself up as a lightning rod in a stormy sky, but I intend to hide behind the four thousand men who comprised our study. The research seems conclusive.

But while I'm at it, I may need to step on some more toes. I suspect that the majority of my audience for this book is securely married and as far away from the divorce court as from the grave. But let me propose this question: Even though you may not be divorced, are you living as if you were? Are you in some lifeless coexistent relationship with your wife for the sake of the kids? Being married does not automatically make you an effective dad. What made our effective fathers different is that they were cultivating strong marriages in which they and their wives were growing together in love and trust and communication. If you want to become a better father, you will need to devote energy to becoming a better husband, too.

A strong marriage does much to help you fulfill your fathering role. We can break this fifth secret of effective fathers into two components: marital interaction and parental discussion. Marital interaction is simply the loving bond that you have with your wife. When you strengthen it, you provide an atmosphere of security in your home in which your children can grow. You also model what an effective marriage looks like, and thus determine how your children perceive marriage and whether they themselves will eventually be successful when they get married.

Parental discussion is the second fathering component that includes your wife. When you discuss your children with your wife and get feedback from her on your fathering, you create a parenting team that uses your collective wisdom in raising the children.

One of the Best Things You Can Do for Your Kids

Marital interaction means focusing on your children by focusing on your wife. The action may seem indirect, but your children will be the direct beneficiaries.

There are plenty of studies that document the connection between a strong marriage and effective fathering. One study of school-aged children and their parents revealed that marital quality is a predictor of a father's ability to give positive feedback.[6] If the father had low marital satisfaction, he was more likely to be intrusive in father-child interactions and give less positive feedback to his children. The extreme of negative findings was a 1987 study of 129 incestuous fathers. Marital failure among sexual offenders was one of the distinguishing characteristics that led to the sexual abuse of children.[7]

A study in Israel showed that a father's marital satisfaction was influential in fathers who viewed fatherhood as a self-enriching experience.[8] Glen Elder, the man who did the study on families who experienced the Great Depression, discovered that a close and compatible marriage mitigated some of the ill effects of economic deprivation, particularly for sons. In other words, a close marriage was able to provide security for boys despite massive economic disaster.[9]

While we might be inclined to separate husband-wife and father-child interactions as two different relationships, these studies say that's impossible. The quality of marital life goes a long way toward determining our communication with our children, the sexual protection of our children, our commitment to and satisfaction with our children, and the ability of our children to handle crises. These are only a few of the connections.

Do you love your kids? Well, one of the best things you can do for them is to love their mother. The main benefit to your children of good marital interaction between you and your wife is an atmosphere of security.

I can picture a girl coming home from school. She leaves her best friend at the corner and walks up the driveway to her house. Her pink-and-green knapsack bounces against her shoulder blades and sends her blonde ponytail flying out behind her. She approaches the door and her hand reaches for the doorknob. At this point, one of two things can happen. The little hand turns the knob without a moment's thought, and the girl steps briskly across the threshold. "I'm home!" she says. She drops her knapsack in the middle of the hallway, as children often do, and then goes bounding into the kitchen for a hug and an after-school snack.

In the other scenario, back on the front porch, the little hand hesitates on the doorknob, turning it slowly, so the latch doesn't yet slip. This little girl is thinking, *What will this be like today?* She leans close, with her ear almost touching the door, listening.

Getting Away to Get It Together

Bill Wellons writes, "In the past eight years my wife and I have learned the tremendous value of biannually to annually escaping the rut of routine activities and busy schedules by planning some time away to think. More than any other single tool, this getaway game plan has helped to keep our marriage fresh and vital as we seek God's will worked out through our marriage and family."

To assist other couples in having their own weekend getaway retreats, Bill and his wife, Carolyn, have written a workbook entitled *Getting Away to Get It Together*. Over the course of a weekend, you and your wife work through six exercises that help you talk without interruption, remember various milestones, balance priorities as a team, and plan out how to work on your relationship until the time of your next getaway. A pre-getaway checklist insures that your kids are cared for and your expectations are realistic.

According to Bill and Carolyn, a great getaway experience:

- Requires an unpressured block of time (ideally a minimum of two nights and portions of three days).
- Balances structure and spontaneity in scheduling.
- Allows some time apart for individual refreshment.
- Focuses on the enjoyment of a process together even more than the finished product.
- Emphasizes putting your marriage on the offensive rather than the defensive to life's issues.
- Demands that you do some thinking about the past, present, and future.
- Must be in an environment that will stimulate romance and relaxation.
- Requires an investment in each other that is well worth the money you will spend.

To order *Getting Away to Get It Together*, simply write Bill Wellons at 12061 Hinson Road, Little Rock, Arkansas 72212.

She might hear her mom and dad—the two most important people in her life, the two people she loves the most—fighting uncontrollably. Or, when the latch finally slips and the door swings open, it might reveal what she has been fearing for months now: Daddy's gone. He's taken an apartment for a couple months until he can find something more permanent as he waits for the divorce to go through. The last thing this little girl wants to do in the face of such fear is to open the door and enter this home.

Both of these scenarios happen every day in homes across America.

Rebecca is a girl who did open her front door one day to find that her life had changed forever. She was in the sixth grade when she wrote an essay for the National Center for Fathering:

Everybody in my family has had to put up a lot with all the things that have gone wrong. One thing about this divorce is that when I go over to my friends' house to spend the night or something, their fathers usually come in and say good night, not good-bye. When my father comes over to get something, and he is about to leave, he always comes over and kisses me on the cheek and then says "good-bye," and walks out. And it hurts a lot. Sometimes I want to just cry. I wish this never happened. . . .

This little girl feels the pain so deeply that she is attuned to such subtle nuances as the difference between *good night* and *good-bye*. The atmosphere of her childhood, even though her father sees her regularly and shows her physical affection, is an atmosphere of pain.

Compare that to what Tasha, a fourth grader, wrote in her essay: "He treats my mom very nicely, which makes me feel wanted." Kids *do* notice, and the notions about marriage that they take with them from childhood will have ramifications throughout their adult lives.

The father and mother are the leaders of the household. They originated the family, and all the children take their cues from them. Though the marriage is not the only relationship in the family, it is certainly the first and the most important. What would happen in a business if, for some reason, the two controlling partners started feuding? What if these two presiding officers suddenly proclaimed competing visions for the company or developed an intense personality conflict? Regardless of how ardently these two partners individually communicated their commitment to the company's employees, the entire company would still suffer. Morale would drop. Everyone would begin to worry about job security. Some mid-level executives would bail out. The emotional atmosphere of the entire organization mirrors the quality of its most important relationship.

But the family is more than just an *organization*; it is an *organism* where husband and wife have become one and where the children are our flesh and blood. This makes the relationship all the more crucial. What would happen to our entire body if our brain and our heart decided not to interact with each other in a healthy manner? What if the brain decided not to remind the heart to pump anymore? What if the heart chose not to feed blood to the brain? What hope would there be for any of the other parts of the body, regardless of how committed the brain and heart might be to their own well-being?

If the atmosphere of the marriage is distrust, the atmosphere of the family is distrust. If the atmosphere of the marriage is anger, the atmosphere of the child rearing is anger. If the atmosphere of the marriage is noncommunication, the atmosphere in which the children grow is silence and foreboding.

On the other hand, if the atmosphere of the marriage is love, the whole family will absorb that love. Children who have two parents who love each other have great soil in which to take root. Their house radiates with a sun that nurtures growth. *A strong marriage breeds security.* The child does not need to fear that the foundation of her life—her parents' marriage—is suddenly going to shake and buckle and split apart.

Like all secrets of effective fathers, strong marital interaction continues to bear fruit in a child's life long after the child has left

125

home. Parents who have a strong marriage are also *modeling* strong marital interaction. All children are born as bachelors and bachelorettes. The first impression they have of marriage is what they observe in their own parents' union. They're watching you. They're taking notes. Your sons, however subconsciously, are asking the question: What does it mean to be a husband? They are also trying to figure out who these creatures called women are, and they are looking to you to see how you perceive them and what respect you give to them. Your daughters also have their eye on you. To submit to another in the mystery of marriage can be a fearful thing; your daughters are asking themselves how well their mother fared in the deal.

Christine is a thirty-six-year-old acquaintance of mine who recently asked her mother, "Do you think Dad treats you well?" Her mom told a story that she'd been dying to tell someone, of one evening years before when she'd come home from work after having been chewed out by her boss. She had stood over the stove, trying to cook supper, but couldn't contain her tears. Her husband was watching her from the table, but he didn't even bother to ask, "What's wrong?" Christine told her mom in reply to the story, "With pain like that, why would anyone want to get married?" To this date Christine hasn't. She says she would like to marry, and she's even been proposed to, but something holds her back.

Your modeling of a loving marriage influences many of your children's perspectives and practices in their own marriages. Before he or she marries, it influences your child's view of whether marriage is even desirable. After the wedding, it helps your child develop a healthy understanding of what a husband or wife does or says, feels or thinks. It will also affect your child's decisions about whether to stick it out through the tough times that his marriage will inevitably face. It's easy to see how children of divorce are more likely to divorce their spouses than children who grew up in two-parent homes. They wonder about this thing called marriage, and they try to get a handle on why some people talk about it with a sparkle in their eye, while others set

Teamwork

The heart of marital interaction is teamwork—a man and wife "working together for a common goal." And yet that is almost a cliché and such an inadequate way to describe teamwork. In order to approach a fitting definition, I have to refer to images of teamwork. It's the way a basketball player can pull down a rebound and, almost without looking, fire a pass down court, knowing exactly where his point guard will be. It's a shortstop and second baseman when a double-play ball is hit, moving instinctively, with perfect timing, relaying the ball to first just in time to nip the runner, but getting him every time.

A better illustration of teamwork occurred in the little town of Lake Placid, New York, when the U.S. Hockey team won the gold. As I think about it now, I can't name one of those hockey players, and yet what they did is something many people in this country will never forget. In December of that year, *Sports Illustrated* changed its year-end award from "Sportsman of the Year"—which usually went to Muhammad Ali or Kareem Abdul Jabbar—to "Sports*men* of the Year."

Such teamwork has powerful effects. One man was driving through a rainstorm, listening to the game between Team USA and the Russian team on his car radio. As the final ticks of the clock approached, he pulled to the side of the road, then began yelling and honking from inside his car. He got out in the rain and yelled some more. By now there were eight or nine other drivers who had also pulled over to add their shouts to the chorus. The ten of them huddled together next to the road as the cars and semis splashed by, soaking them, but they didn't care. They were yelling out, in unison, "We beat the Russians!" Things that would never happen ordinarily—ten total strangers dancing and hugging each other next to a highway—but these things become possible when there is teamwork.

Here's how *Sports Illustrated* writer E. M. Swift saw it:

Individually they were fine, dedicated sportsmen. Some will have excellent pro hockey careers. Others will bust. But collectively, they were a transcendent

127

> *lot. For seven months they pushed each other on and pulled each other along, from rung to rung, until for two weeks in February they—a bunch of unheralded amateurs—became the best hockey team in the world. The best team. The whole was greater than the sum of its parts by a mile. And they were not just a team; they were innovative and exuberant and absolutely unafraid to succeed. They were a perfect reflection of how Americans wanted to perceive themselves.*
>
> *They owned the whole country for a while. It just made you want to pick up your television set and take it to bed with you. It really made you feel good.*
>
> I believe that this is the perfect reflection of how every *husband-wife* team wants to perceive themselves. The ones who will be celebrating for the rest of their lives will be your children. Together as a couple, you can really make them feel good.
>
> In 1981 ABC aired a movie about Team USA called *Miracle on Ice*. And it truly was a miracle. It was David beating Goliath; the '69 Miracle Mets.
>
> And that's the kind of phenomenon you can experience in your household. Just look around. The odds are stacked up a hundred to one against you in today's world. But the whole of your marriage really is greater than the sum of its parts. It's time to allow God to work in your kids through the miracle of teamwork.
>
> E. M. Swift, "A Reminder of What We Can Be," *Sports Illustrated*, 22/29 December 1980, 30-46.

their jaw and mutter bitter expletives. As parents, we model our levels of commitment or apathy to the institution of marriage.

If you were to ask fathers, "How would you like your children to turn out?" most would talk about their becoming good citizens, respectable persons, successful and satisfied in their careers. Most fathers would also admit that they'd like their children to marry good spouses and be happy in their marriages. Some fathers are even looking forward to grandchildren and want these little ones to grow up in an atmosphere of love and cooperation. You as a father have a great deal to say about these outcomes, even about the home life of your yet-unborn grandchildren, but you are not allowed to say it or write it in a will; you have to *model* it instead. Love your wife, and it is likely your son will love his. Create an atmosphere of love through strong marital interaction in your home, and it's likely your grandchildren will grow up in one too.

Teamwork

The other aspect of fathering that involves your wife is parental discussion. If marital interaction is where you and your wife come together as one to focus on each other, parental discussion is where you come together—also as one—to focus on your children.

Here are the questions that our effective fathers were able to answer in the affirmative:

1. Do you discuss your children's development with your wife?

2. Do you discuss your children's problems with your wife?

3. Do you discuss goals for each child with your wife?

4. Do you discuss your frustrations as a parent with your wife?

If you were able also to answer these questions with a yes, then you've discovered that of all your fathering assets—your secret weapons, if you will—the one that ranks at the top of the list is your wife. You've discovered that you are not alone, and also that you and your wife can form a parenting team that can work effectively for your children's benefit.

We asked fathers in our surveys, "What person has contributed most to helping you overcome difficulties in your fathering?" Some men listed their pastors, others listed their male

129

friends or even their dad. Some men listed psychologist James Dobson. But the overwhelming answer given to our question was "my wife."

The synergy itself is pretty remarkable. Women have done an admirably heroic job of raising the past few generations of children. In many cases, they've had to do it by themselves, as many men relinquished the role of father and were blind to the long-term satisfactions of being actively involved in the family. But however good a mother might be as a mother, she can't also be a father. Only a father can be a father. As men return to the home, like many are doing today, it is not simply the addition of a second parent. A mother is a mother but she is also a wife, a wife who, through discussion, can assist her husband to be a better father.

This coincides with advice from the seventeenth century. As noted earlier, Puritan author William Whately suggested that in parenting "two eyes see more than one."[10] Another common Puritan epigram reminded fathers that a wife is your eye to see when you are not there, she is your hand to touch, she is your ear to hear. In simple words, she is a living person who can gain information about your children that you cannot gain. Hers are the additional insightful eyes that fathers need.

Actually, there are three things that your wife can provide you with through parental discussion. First, she can provide you with additional data about your children. She will be places with your kids that you will not be. She may be at home during the day, while you are at work. She may be with your daughter at softball practice, while you are driving your son on his paper route. But when you both get together again, and the kids have quieted down for the evening, you get to ask, "So how's Susie doing?" and your wife will tell you the stories. You gain that much more knowledge about who your kids are.

Your wife can also provide you with a different perspective on your children. If you are sitting on the couch, and your wife is in the recliner, you might both be looking at the same child playing on the living room floor, but you will be seeing the child differently. In a sense, you only see one portion of your child's life—your perspective. Your wife has a different perspective. It can be quite illuminating when you compare notes. Ask your wife, "So what do you make of Jonathan's report card?" or "Did you think it was strange the way Tammy introduced us to her friends?" You will particularly want to seek your wife's insights when it comes to relating with your growing daughters.

My wife's ability for special insight into our children—and her husband!—was driven home for me recently. I think I've mentioned my system of organization: I put things in piles. Everyone in my household knows it, and I justify it by saying I'm research-oriented, and it's an important skill for my research. One day Dee came to me and told me that the reason there was a shortage of towels in our house was, she had just found, that no less than twelve of them were in various bunches of things on Sarah's bedroom floor. "What?" I said. "Twelve towels! I can't believe that! She should know better than to. . . . "

I paused when I noticed one corner of my wife's mouth curling into a grin. She put her finger on her chin and looked at me thoughtfully. "Hmmm. Acts like someone else I know."

There I was, ready to jump all over Sarah and cause a minor family crisis, when it was clear to Dee that this could be easily explained and excused. I now realize that Sarah has inherited my piling gene.

Regular discussion with your wife can also yield tips on how to improve your own parenting skills. One research study reported that a father's lack of fathering skills is often linked to increased marital conflict.[11] The reason that these fathers lack parenting skills is that they shut themselves off from the most knowledgeable teachers of parenting: their wives. Ask for advice and listen. Also ask for feedback. It's easy to be blind to our own strengths and weaknesses. Sometimes the most profitable question you can ask is simply, "Honey, how am I doing?"

A father who discusses his fathering with his wife gains a great deal of confidence. No longer is he simply muddling through, hoping to avoid any major blunders before the kids leave home. At the very least, he is learning how to father. Mistakes he makes are simply lessons to be learned, and he does learn his lessons, having talked through them thoroughly with his spouse. Parental discussion also leads naturally to setting goals for your children and creating plans for your parenting. You and your wife can decide issues beforehand, such as at what age you will allow your daughters to begin wearing makeup or what rules will govern the use of the family car. You will find yourself making decisions beforehand when you can think wisely and objectively, before the heat of the battle rages and saps your confidence.

I am now working on another book, this one coauthored with Nancy Swihart and tentatively entitled *Wives Helping Husbands Become Better Fathers.* Poor Nancy has been besieged. Her part of the writing keeps getting interrupted with requests for speaking engagements and articles on the topic. Women are generally anxious to invite their husbands to be part of a parenting team.

Occasionally I meet a woman who seems overly protective of her parental role, even resentful that her husband has begun to encroach upon her territory. If your wife seems to create a hedge between you and the children, if you ask a question about the kids and she responds, "Why do you want to know?" the best gift you can give her is empathy. In many cases, women are also working through issues from a fatherless childhood. Fathers are not people they've learned to trust, and unfortunately this distrust can be transferred to you, the father of her children. We may also have to admit that we've earned some of that distrust, particularly if we've dumped the kids on our wives during those years we've been off conquering the world.

Any reluctance on a wife's part to invite her husband into the parental team demonstrates the importance of having strong marital interaction accompany parental discussion. If you attempt to discuss with your wife how to meet the needs of your children without paying attention to how you can also meet her needs, you are *using* your wife. She will feel like a glorified nanny, hired to be a steward of your greater interests. If instead you express your growing commitment to her sincerely and regularly, your wife will eagerly join you as you work together on a great common interest—your children. You will have discovered a unique and invaluable treasure.

Enhancing the Marital Bond

Having a plan to enhance your marital bond is as important as having a plan to interact with your children. There are numerous helpful books and seminars that can enable you to enrich your marriage. Ask your wife, your pastor, or your male friends for suggestions. But in the remainder of this chapter, let me provide those practical tips that most closely link your marriage and your fathering.

Repeat your wedding vows often, so your wife and children can hear them regularly. I think I saw it on an old "All in the Family" rerun, though if I didn't, I can easily imagine Archie and Edith in this scene: Archie is in his favorite chair, reading the newspaper. His wife, Edith, is on the couch silently knitting. She keeps looking up at her husband, and finally she just has to ask:

"Archie, do you love me?"

Archie drops his paper. "What kind of question is that?" he asks.

"Do you still love me?"

"Of course I still love you. Why do you ask?"

"You never tell me that you love me," Edith replies.

"Oh, that's not true," Archie responds. "On our wedding night, I said, 'Edith, I love you.'"

"But I gotta hear it more than that."

"Whaddaya mean? I told you once. That should be enough. If it ever changes, I'll let you know."

Our wives need to hear us reaffirm our commitment to them regularly. When we made our vows at the wedding ceremony, if we used the traditional vows, our wives heard us pledge our faithfulness "for richer, for poorer, in sickness and in health, from this day forward, till death do us part." The wedding ceremony had us verbalize our commitment all at once, but marriage lets us separate those vows into more understandable and demonstrable pieces. During periods of richness and health, we get to say, "Honey, things are really going well, and I want you to know that I can't think of another woman I would choose to enjoy all of this with." During periods of poverty and sickness, we repeat our vows: "Sweetheart, we may be struggling right now, but I want you to know that I'm going to stick it out with you." We also repeat our vows "from this day forward": "Well, honey, here you are turning the big 'four-oh,' but I have to tell you, you are more attractive to me now than when we first married," or "Sweetheart, the kids have all left home now, but I still have you, and that's enough. I love you." Our wives need to hear us repeat our vows over the years and in as many different situations as possible (menopause being an important one). And we have to admit, we kind of like it when they do the same for us!

Our children also need to hear us repeat our vows to our wives. The neighborhood where we live has a number of families who have experienced or even now are going through divorce. My kids play with their kids, visit their homes, and bring them into ours. Your children are probably similar: all kids know some kids whose parents have divorced.

One time, my wife, Dee, and I had let our checking account run a little low. I had to make a major purchase and had given Dee another check to deposit in the account so that I could write the check for the purchase. We were sitting in the living room the next day. The kids were playing around us. It suddenly struck me to ask about the deposit, so I asked Dee if she had deposited the check.

Her eyebrows rose, and the right corner of her mouth tightened. "Oh, no," she said.

134

She had forgotten. The check was still in her purse.

Now, I suppose I could have told myself that these things happen and that I had certainly forgotten enough things in my lifetime. Instead, my mind was focused on the overdraft, the fifteen-dollar penalty, and the fact that this had happened before.

"Oh, for crying out loud, Dee! You were out running errands. Didn't you think about going to the bank?" I went on to make a few more insensitive comments. Eventually, Dee's eyes began to fill with tears.

But we both immediately forgot our argument (or *my* argument) when we noticed that everything around us had gotten deathly quiet. We looked at our kids, and they were staring at us with looks that I can only describe as fearful.

Dee and I hadn't been yelling at each other. We hadn't been screaming and throwing things. Although I was being insensitive, we both knew that this was just another one of those disagreements that pop up in marriage. We both knew that all would eventually be covered in mutual forgiveness.

Our children, however, were wide-eyed. *This is what divorce looks like,* they were telling themselves. Hannah and Sarah were exchanging glances. They were both thinking the same thing: *Cassie Greenwood!* Cassie is a friend of theirs whose parents are in financial straits. The Greenwoods are contemplating bankruptcy, and the tension has already pushed them to a temporary separation. My kids heard Dee and me discussing the check, they sensed some tension in the air, and they concluded, *Mom and Dad are going to divorce each other.*

Dee and I were surprised how easily our children jumped to the conclusion that we were going to divorce, despite our having what we consider to be a strong marriage. It reminded us that we need to repeat our vows regularly before our children. We did right then and there. "Your mom and I might have our disagreements on occasion, but we also know that we made some vows before God, and that these vows were witnessed by your grandparents and your aunts and uncles. We are not going to divorce. We love each other. I know that the Greenwoods may be going through a divorce, but we're going to be different."

Discuss marriage and divorce with your children. You may

135

want to dig your wedding album out of the drawer and flip through it with the kids. After they get done remarking about how much hair you had back then and laughing about the width of your tuxedo's lapels, you can begin to tell them why you married their mom and what you think of the vows you made. Dee and I have a Valentine's Day tradition. We gather the kids around, and Dee and I sit close to each other. Together we tell them about our love for each other, and then we pray aloud for each of them and for their future spouses, as God so allows (although Joel is at the age where marriage is a pretty repugnant thought!).

Show affection for your wife in front of your kids. Voicing your commitment is one thing; demonstrating it is another. Word and deed together provide convincing proof: Dad loves Mom and all is right with the universe.

I guess I don't need to give any more practical advice here. You know what to do: a peck on the cheek, a nice hug when you arrive home, a soothing back rub, sharing space on the couch, and maybe even an occasional long kiss that is passionate enough to embarrass your teenagers. ("Mom, Dad, please. There are children in the room.")

This advice concerning PDAs—Public Displays of Affection—must be accompanied by this warning: Do not practice in public what you are not practicing in private. That is the essence of pharisaism. If you are not regularly showing affection to your wife in private, she will begin to suspect that your public shows of affection are simply shows, without any feeling or meaning behind them.

Date your mate. This is a popular phrase. What I like about it is that it is more than just the action of occasionally taking your wife out for special evenings together. It is a philosophy. "Date your mate" is a mind-set in which you seek to treat your wife like you did before you proposed to her.

There was a great deal of tension in dating, which marriage happily relieves. Now you can relax and be yourself. You can revel in the unconditional nature of the marriage commitment.

But there was also a great deal of thrill and earnestness in dating. You weren't taking this girl of your dreams for granted. You were consciously plotting how you could win her heart. You probably had a keen eye for what made her happy. It was a joy to see her every time. Dating your mate means reinstating some of the conditions of your dating relationship. Oh, you probably don't have to ask her father for permission any longer. And that eleven-o'clock curfew is a thing of the past. But revitalize your purpose: to continually rewin your true love's affections. And revive some of the old activities: dinners and movies and walks in the park (with the kids tucked safely away at Grandma's).

Dating your mate can also help your children. Dating will provide its share of tension for them too. There will be one day when your son will pace back and forth in front of the phone just like you did when you were his age. He'll be rehearsing a speech in his head about being in this girl's math class and about if she's "not doing anything Friday night." Finally, he'll get up enough courage to dial six of the seven numbers of her phone number. It can be a gut-wrenching experience. You can talk your children through their first date and let them know what to expect, but you can also demonstrate a lot for them. Your kids will be watching the way you open the car door for your wife. They'll be listening when you compliment her on how nice she looks in that new dress.

Take your kids with you when you go shopping for a gift for your wife. Your anniversary. Her birthday. Valentine's Day. Christmas. "No special occasion; I just wanted to surprise you."

Your kids will be witnessing your giving expression to your love. They will see you esteeming your wife in her position. When you solicit their gift suggestions, you not only get some good ideas, but you communicate to them that their mother is important; not just any gift will do—you want to give her something suited especially to her. (The best hint I've heard of late: Women don't consider anything they have to plug in to be a gift!)

Don't make your wife suffer unnecessarily for the sake of the children. Make your wife's basic needs a priority in your finances. I'm amazed at how quickly our kids go through clothes. We buy Sarah a pair of Levis and she complains, "But they're too long. Look how baggy they are." We tell her that she'll grow into them, but she doesn't; she grows *out* of them. The next time I see her in those jeans, the bottom cuff is almost visibly inching up her calf. Time for a new pair. In some years of a child's life, you actually replace an entire wardrobe within a twelve-month period. I'm conscious of the financial strain of spending money on my children's clothes, but I also have to remind myself, in the process, not to forget Dee. It is good for our wives, if that is their desire, to buy new clothes, to look nice, to feel good about their femininity.

Too often we forget what our wives need because we are too conscious of what our children need. We assume that our wives should sacrifice because, after all, that's what parents do. It's good not to verbalize that sentiment though, because your wife may well tell you about nine months of pregnancy and sixteen-odd hours of labor multiplied by one-too-many kids. They will be right: they've suffered enough. When we fail to attend to our wives' basic needs, we go too far. I know of men who have postponed surgery for their wives so they could get braces for their kids instead.

Healthy marital interaction and thorough parental discussion are the means by which you invite your wife to help multiply your fathering skills. Together they make up the fifth secret of effective fathers. In many marriages, the husband and father is more in love with his children than he is with his wife. My friend Tom came through the divorce that he initiated smelling pretty sweet. The judge was impressed with his custody arguments, and even though he didn't give Tom the children, he did remark how good a father Tom seemed to be. Since the divorce, Tom has not missed a child-support payment. He makes wide use of his access rights and remains involved in his children's lives by attending parent-teacher conferences at school and cheering them on at their soccer games. No one can accuse Tom of not loving his children.

Neither can anyone accuse Jeff of not loving his children. Jeff is still married to Kristi, but only remains so "for the sake of the kids." He plays passionately with the children in the backyard but does not bring that same passion into the bedroom.

These men love their children. There's no doubt about that. But I've asked them both: "What if I told you that one of the best ways to love your children is to love their mother? Would you love your children enough to tell your wife 'I do'?"

We need to be passionate about the one who provided us with the opportunity to be a father in the first place.

Husbands, love your children's mother.

Eight

SECRET 6:
Active
Listening

In 1987, evangelist Luis Palau visited Manhattan, Kansas, to conduct a week-long evangelistic campaign. "Hope for the Heartland," he called it.

Luis told how he had just completed an around-the-world trip during which he had managed to visit every continent except Antarctica and Australia in two months' time. Before he left, he had asked God to give him a mental picture for each continent that would give him insight into what was happening spiritually in these places. Luis described these images.

Europe, he said, impressed him as a beautiful woman dressed in all her finery. But when you see her, she is lying in a gutter of poverty and degradation. She has the riches of Christianity and yet is still starving. Africa came to Luis's mind as a burning fire, blazing wildly. The gospel was spreading miraculously throughout the continent, but cults were also springing up amid the flames.

Luis remembered Asia as a young virgin waiting to be wooed. She was ready to be drawn in by whomever would give her attention.

When Luis thought of the USSR and the Eastern bloc, the

143

picture that came to his mind was of a motel room, locked from the inside with a latch. The door was slightly ajar, and eyes peered out past the chain latch, wanting to know more of what was on the outside.

Finally, he said that South America appeared to him as an orphan child, a half-naked boy wandering hungrily through the streets, asking for someone to feed him.

The pictures were vivid and meaningful.

Afterward, I was able to meet with Luis in his motel room. I asked him if he had come up with an image of America.

"Oh, yes," he said. He closed his eyes, trying to recapture the picture. "America is like a man standing on the corner of some busy street in some large city. Cars are humming by, horns are blaring, people are talking, and the street light has just turned from 'Don't Walk' to 'Walk'. But the man doesn't move. He's confused by all the noise. He can't seem to hear what he needs to hear."

I've thought often about this encounter with Luis Palau. I've thought that instead of touring the continents, I might take a walk with him through my neighborhood.

"I think, Luis," I would say, pointing to a large two-story home, "that this is a European home. The parents bring home two fairly substantial incomes, but their three kids are starved for their time and affection.

"Over here, the red-brick ranch-style is, to my mind, a Soviet home. In fact, look, see that little face peering through the curtains. There's a lot of pain, a lot of dysfunction in that home. The kids all wonder what a normal home life is like."

Luis and I would walk around the block, with me pointing out Asian homes and South American homes. At the end of our tour, I would say, "See, Luis, a whole world of families in this one-block radius."

However, I have a feeling that Luis Palau would turn to me at that point and say, "Perhaps. But this is America. And these are American homes. I still see the same picture: men standing in their living rooms like pedestrians at a street corner. They are

ACTIVE LISTENING

Effective fathers showed higher scores in verbal interaction with their children by giving them full attention when they were speaking. This scale also included items such as: allowing children to disagree, and not becoming angry; creating an atmosphere of caring and acceptance that encourages children to share their ideas; and listening closely to their concerns.

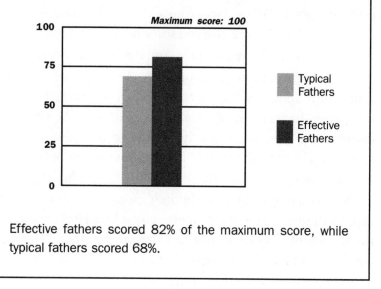

Effective fathers scored 82% of the maximum score, while typical fathers scored 68%.

surrounded by noise—some of their own making—and they are finding it hard to distinguish the tiny voices of their children. They can't hear. They don't listen to what they need to hear."

Finding Meaning in the Mayhem

Our homes can be very noisy places. The television blares. The washing machine rattles and bumps. The microwave beeps. The kids, with their full slate of activities, come rumbling through the living room and out the front door. But there's other noise. There's the checkbook, which, even when we shove it into the briefcase or throw it into the drawer, still manages to voice its demands: "You gotta pay the bills. You gotta pay the bills." Our job stands outside and taps incessantly on the glass of the windows: "Hey, pay attention to me. Pay attention to me." The clock in the hallway ticks the minutes loudly enough to echo against the walls and remind us of all we have to do and of how little time we have in which to do it.

And we add our own noise. The only way, we figure, to gain control of the hubbub is to shout above it loudly enough to be heard. So we throw in our two cents: "Do this!" we scream. "Don't do that!" we yell. "When I was your age . . . " "You know what you need to do. . . ." "Let me give you some advice. . . . "

A home can be a noisy place. And that's unfortunate.

It's unfortunate because beneath all the noise, there are some softly spoken whispers that need to be heard. These are tiny voices that occasionally scamper like unseen mice from the floorboards. They peep quietly, "Listen to me, please. I have something important to say." But they often go unnoticed amid the cacophony. These are the tiny voices of your children.

Now you may think your children are anything but soft-spoken. It's dinnertime, and I tell Joel to go get his sisters, who are in the basement. Joel walks two feet toward the stairs. "Hannah, Sarah!" he hollers. "Time for dinner."

"I could have done that," I say.

And Micah isn't particularly quiet. "I was in the hospital once," he tells me.

"I know, Micah. I was there with you."

"My leg was broke in two places."

"Yeah, I remember."

"The doctor put a mask over my face."

He's told me the story a hundred times.

Our children may not seem quiet. But the tiny voices I'm talking about don't come from their larynx. These particular whispers begin deeper—from the heart. In a hundred different ways our children try to communicate to us who they are, what they feel, what they fear, whom they love, how they think, what they hope, why they cry, when they laugh, where they hurt.

These are intimate things, and like anything intimate they are rarely shouted. More often this information is whispered, with the mouth close to the ear. And it is whispered to you, the father, because you are the most important man in the world. Your children want you to know who they are, so that you can accept them fully. Your children want to tell you where it hurts, so you can fix it.

It's time for a confession. (Perhaps this is why this chapter is hidden in the back of the book.) I have trouble actively listening to my children. With five kids and their friends running through the house, one of my favorite remarks is, "Let's all be quiet for a while." I like a quiet household.

A friend of mine has mistakenly told his kids to be permanently quiet. "Children are to be seen and not heard," he quotes. Jon has mistakenly believed silence is a mark of being spiritual. Yet, if he forces his kids to be silent for the next fifteen years, those kids won't know how to speak, let alone how to be heard by their father.

Too often the important tiny voices of our children get lost beneath adult noise. But there's a lot we can do to turn down the decibels. For example, we can turn off the TV and put away distractions. Most important, we can train ourselves to be slow to speak and quick to listen. We can file away our lectures for another day and let our children speak instead. Some noise may seem beyond our control—the checkbook grumbling in the briefcase, our jobs pounding on the window panes. But even then, we can learn to tune out the noise and focus our attention for those times when we especially need to listen to our children.

Effective fathers have learned the discipline of actively listening to their children. It is the sixth secret of effective fathers.

Selective Hearing

We often accuse children of selective hearing. I have heard one cynical theory which claims that when a father starts to give a command, the adult voice apparently switches into a frequency that dogs can hear but children cannot.

Sarah runs to the door. I yell after her, "Don't slam the door."

Bam!

I sit down with Joel. "Joel, I thought I told you that you weren't allowed to go outside until you finished your homework."

"I'm sorry, Dad," he says. "I thought you were talking to Hannah."

"Hannah?! I was looking right at you. I even used your name."

"I'm sorry. I guess I didn't hear you."

I would like to bemoan this selective hearing of my children more, but I'm afraid it's too easy for me to be guilty of the same trait. There are so many noises surrounding a father—pressures and demands, schedules and to-do lists. At times, these noises seem to crescendo and drown out everything else, but the fact is that at any given moment, we *choose* what we want to give our attention to.

Put this book down for just a moment and listen to the sounds around you.

What did you hear? Was the fluorescent light humming? Was a fly buzzing across the windowpane? Was there traffic out on the street? All these noises were occurring even before you stopped to listen to them. If you did not notice them before, it was because you *chose* to focus your attention on the words of this page.

At any given time, we can choose to listen to our children. Unfortunately, we as fathers too often do not. Think of the typical media portrayals of the father. Dad is at the breakfast table hidden behind the financial section of the newspaper, only the slightly balding top of his head visible. The kids come downstairs and begin fighting over the milk and cereal.

"Dad, Scott won't give me the milk carton."

A voice comes from behind the newspaper: "Scott, listen to your sister."

Skills of Attentive Listening

Face your child squarely. This is a basic posture of involvement. It usually says, "I'm available to you; I choose to be with you."

Adopt an open posture. Crossed arms and legs can be signs of lessened involvement or availability, while an open posture can be a sign that you're open to your child and to what he or she has to say.

Put yourself on your child's level by squatting down, and if possible, leaning toward him. This communicates, "I'm with you; I want to know more about you."

Maintain good eye contact. This makes many people in our society uneasy, but have you ever talked to someone whose eyes seem to be looking at everything in the room but you? If so, you know how it feels when someone seems reluctant to be involved in your conversation. Don't let your child experience this from you.

Stay relaxed as you listen. If you fidget nervously as your child is talking to you, she will wonder what's making you that way and may get the feeling you'd rather be somewhere else.

Learn to read your child's nonverbal behavior. Watch her posture, body movements, and gestures; notice her frowns, smiles, raised eyebrows, twisted lips, and the like; listen to her voice quality, pitch, intensity, emphases, pauses, and inflections. Quite often how your child says something will tell you more that what she is saying.

Give your child nonverbal feedback by nodding, making your eyes light up, or raising your eyebrows. These small signals will reaffirm your listening involvement and may encourage your child to keep explaining his feelings in greater detail.

Respond to your child by restating in your own words what she has told you. This will not only show your child that you are indeed understanding what she is saying; it will also give her the opportunity to say, "Yes, that's it exactly," or "No, what I really mean is . . . " It will almost always lead to more successful communication.

The goal of listening is understanding.

Adapted from Gerard Egan, *The Skilled Helper* (Monterey, CA: Brooks/Cole Publishing Co., 1986), 72-81.

149

"Dad, cheerleading tryouts are today, and I think I've got a good chance of making the squad."

"Hmm, that's nice," the voice says.

The kids look at each other. The teenage boy ventures with a wry smile, "Hey, Dad, I've robbed three convenience stores and think I may do a fourth on my way to school today."

"Good for you, Son," the voice says.

Even when the media dads are more attentive, they aren't necessarily listening any more effectively. The trademark of the sensitive dad has become the wise and caring lecture. Hugh Beaumont sits on the edge of his son's bed and tells Wally why he shouldn't beat up on Beaver. Robert Young gathers his clan and proves that father knows best by dispensing pearls of wisdom, insights that clear up situations and defuse crises. Bill Cosby takes one of the Huxtable kids into the kitchen and over a bottle of apple juice tells the kid how it is.

Now, there is certainly room for a well-timed lecture. Fathers who speak wisdom to their children are faithfully fulfilling their roles of educating the kids and equipping them for the world. The problem is that we've let the lecture become our stock in trade. It's what we all aspire to: that one perfectly eloquent and learned speech that communicates our deep love for our children and at the same time teaches them the secrets of living life before God. Our kids cry out, "Yes, O wise one, you're right. We understand." Our wives beam at us. We knowingly nod our heads. We have reached the pinnacle of fatherhood!

But this is not what effective fathers do. Oh, sure, they've been known to give a lecture or two in their lifetime. More often, though, they simply listen. Even when they do lecture, they have listened first, and what they have heard tells them what to say.

Fathers need to learn to listen. Children need to be heard. And children respond to the attention. The National Center for Fathering sponsors essay contests. Kids can write about most anything, but often they write about fathers who listen:

> "My father is the person that if you need a shoulder to lean on, he'll be there . . . the person who listens to what some-

body has to say about family problems." (Joey, fourth grade)

"He always listens to my side of the story." (Tasha, fourth grade)

"He's always there when I need him. I can talk to him about things that are going on in my life." (Ruth, sixth grade)

"This year I had my problem with my knees. My dad has been very understanding and willing to listen. He has helped me to realize that even if I can't play in sports, I can still have a good time." (Jason, sixth grade)

"Since my dad bought a full-bred German Shepherd dog, it gives us a chance to be alone in the car going to dog shows. We share our thoughts of what we feel about things. My dad means more than a pen pal." (Timothy, sixth grade)

"He's the type of guy that you can talk to about school, other boys or just plain girlfriends." (Scott, seventh grade)

By contrast, we also received this description from a seminary student in Minnesota:

"Sometimes it's like he's got a mouth but no ears—lots of talk about his interests and activities but few if any questions about mine."

If you want to win with your kids, listen! What makes listening so important is that it feeds all our other fathering roles. It is a foundational discipline for fathering activities.

Let me point out several fathering activities and how listening is crucial to each:

Showing affection. Many fathers show affection to their children. They hug them and often say, "I love you." But what sets effective fathers apart from all other dads is that their listening becomes a sign of affection.

151

Actively listening to your kids communicates to them that you consider them special enough to deserve your undivided attention. You are expressing to them that they are worthy of being known and understood.

In Tim Hansel's book *What Kids Need Most in a Dad*, he quotes psychologist and theologian Paul Tournier:

> *It is impossible to overemphasize the immense need humans have to be really listened to, to be taken seriously, to be understood. No one can develop freely in this world and find life full without feeling understood by at least one person.*[1]

Rose is an elderly woman whom I have been caring for over the years. She is ninety-three years old. Each week, when I stop by the rest home where she resides, she insists on telling me her repertoire of stories. The stories are not new; in fact, most of them happened forty or fifty years ago. I have heard them a hundred times. But one time, when she was telling me her stories, I noticed something in the way she was watching me. I could tell that she was no longer thinking about the story at all, but she was seeing if I was still listening. I can only imagine what she was thinking deep down inside: *Ken, I know that I am old and I know I have told these stories so many times that I've begun to mix their details. But if you listen closely, they will tell you who I am. They are all I have. Do I also have your love? Will you love me enough to listen, even when I lapse into gibberish?*

Much of what our children tell us may seem inconsequential. When they begin to speak of how they view the world, their thoughts may be hopelessly inaccurate and may seem silly or shallow or even . . . well, childish. But many times, the value is not in what is said, but in the *saying* of it. The child is heard and knows that he is loved.

If you haven't already guessed, Micah is the storyteller in our family. When we are driving home from a movie, Micah sits happily in the back of the van (so all can hear him) and recounts the entire plot, even though we were all with him in the theater just minutes ago. The next day we'll get another recap: "Dad, wasn't it great that car wrecking into that truck and all those chickens flying around?" There are some things I can learn about Micah even from these rather monotonous rehashings, but for now my point is that it doesn't matter what the words are: Micah is pleased by my listening.

When you listen, you say I love you without even speaking a word.

Knowing your child. We have already discussed how one of the seven secrets of effective fathers is awareness of how our children are specifically developing. An effective father knows his kids: who they are, what their strengths and weaknesses are, what their gifts and talents are, what motivates or discourages them.

How do you gather this information? By listening. You simply look them in the eyes and in your own fashion say, "Tell me about yourself," and then sit back and take it all in.

If a father is involved in his children's lives and is a regular listener to them, there will be times when the information is up front and straightforward. "Dad, I'm really bummed out," your daughter might say as you and she are riding alone in the car. She may reveal to you what has been one of her greatest disappointments. Your knowledge of your daughter in just a short fifteen-minute conversation takes a quantum leap. In the same way, your son might approach you and ask, "Dad, can we talk?" Something happened to his body last night while he slept, and he's a little embarrassed. You listen and learn how quickly your son is becoming a man. These times are those special moments that your children refer to later when they come home to visit and say, "Dad, you remember those talks we used to have?" Actually, such a question is probably a lead-in to another of these special, intimate moments of talking and listening.

But we need to understand that these open, honest moments will never occur unless the father proves himself as a listener during the other moments, where the only thing that seems to be happening is somewhat tedious chitchat. A child who finds his father open to the small things will be more willing to share the large things with him.

And sometimes we learn just as much, if not more, during the off times. After noticing how much Rose, my ninety-three-year-old friend, desired that I listen, I began to listen to her stories more intently. Instead of interrupting to remind her of details, like I had in the past, I let her speak. I found out that the details that I thought she was confused about were actually *new* details or new emphases. She was revealing new information, nuances of who she was and what was important to her. When you are ninety-three, the parts of your life that remain to be colored in are rarely painted with grand strokes of the brush. More often, it requires subtle shading, gradual highlighting, a touch of detail. Only the committed listener can catch the full beauty of that life.

Our children will have their grand strokes, but much of what they reveal about themselves will come quietly, subtly, in unsuspected ways at unsuspected moments.

Motivation. Statistically, strong listening behaviors are usually linked to motivation. When a research questionnaire comes in to the National Center and I see that the man has a high listening score, I usually find that he has a high motivation score too. If his listening score is low, so is his motivation score. They are highly correlated.

Our research has also examined men who claimed they were highly satisfied with their fathering. We set out to find the one quality or skill that was connected most directly to fathering satisfaction. In other words, we wanted to know what one trait most often accompanied fathers' satisfaction. This was interesting: The trait with the highest correlation to fathering satisfaction is verbal interaction. The father who talks with and listens to his children gets the most satisfaction as a dad.

What is it about listening that feeds our motivation as a father? One reason may be that it allows us to experience the purest joy of being in a relationship: intimacy. We get to connect with another human being who is important to us. Another reason may be the honor we feel at being taken in as a confidant. If our children feel loved because we listen, we feel loved in return because they trust us enough to share their deep thoughts and emotions.

Active listening also enhances our motivation because it protects us from that awful sense that our children are concealing deep, dark secrets that they might spring on us at any moment. Fathers who don't listen have good reason to foster such fear. How often is the scene replayed where the child reveals an unexpected crisis? "Why didn't you tell us this before, while there was still time to do something about it?" the angry father demands.

"I tried to," the girl says, in tears, "but you weren't listening."

Active listening does its greatest work for our motivation as fathers by helping relieve us of one of our greatest fears: that we as fathers need to have all the answers. You and I both know we don't have all the answers. Often we feel inadequate to the task of fathering. It may seem ironic to say that listening can relieve this pressure. After all, our tendency is to think that what we don't know won't hurt us. Or that if we don't ask about our children's problems they won't ask us to solve them. But more often than not, our children aren't looking for answers anyway. They are looking for a chance to express themselves, for a listening ear, for a vote of confidence, or for a sign of our love. Sometimes they find their own answers, but wouldn't have done so well if they hadn't used us as a sounding board. Fathers who are on the lecture circuit, as compared to the listening circuit, are under a great deal of pressure. They are under the gun to say wise and memorable things. Yet even when they do speak, they have no assurance that they are heard, because they never stop long enough to listen to an answer to the questions, "Do you understand?" or, "Does this seem relevant to what you are going through?"

155

Turn Down the Noise

You may have noticed that I use the term *active listening*. I do this because the type of listening that is effective is not a passive pursuit. You are actively seeking to understand what your children are thinking and feeling. Sometimes that means you get up out of your chair and turn off the TV. Other times, you even speak in the listening situation, either to ask questions for inquiry or clarification or to repeat something back to your child to make sure you are both on the same wavelength.

Whatever listening is, it is certainly more than letting sound waves bounce off your ear drums. Child psychiatrist Ross Campbell, in his book *How to Really Love Your Child,* calls it "focused attention." He writes,

> *What is focused attention? Focused attention is giving a child our full, undivided attention in such a way that he feels without doubt that he is completely loved. That he is valuable enough in his own right to warrant parents' undistracted watchfulness, appreciation, and uncompromising regard.*

Campbell goes on to claim that focused attention "is so vital in a child's development of self-esteem. And it profoundly affects a child's ability to relate to and love others."[2]

Every year, large corporations pay big bucks to train their key employees in listening skills. Listening translates into efficiency, productivity, and good work relations. It also releases the abilities of all the employees to contribute to the creative solving of any problems the company may have. Except for the congenitally deaf, we are all born hearers. But we are not born listeners. Listening is a discipline that we can learn, at which we can become more proficient. Effective fathers are craftsmen at listening. We can become the same.

If you ever get an opportunity to participate in a listening skills seminar, I would encourage you to jump at the chance. We are taught how to speak and how to write, but rarely do we get any help with listening. Nonetheless, there are a few basic principles of listening that can easily be grasped here. Perhaps we can summarize all of them in one short axiom:

Turn down the noise!

If you want to listen to what your children are saying, then you need to have it quiet enough to hear them. Some of this deafening noise is in our environment; a great deal of it is in our own heads. We need to turn down both if we want to give our kids focused attention.

Turn down the noise by removing physical distractions. When you are attempting to listen to someone, you need to be able to do two things: number one, actually *hear* the words they're saying; and number two, *concentrate* on those words. Consequently, when your children approach you with something to say, it just makes good sense to get up and turn off the TV, stereo, air compressor, or whatever it is in the room that is making noise. Clearing out distractions also means setting aside the magazine you were reading or putting down the project you were working on. You are free to listen.

If I were to ask you, "What is more important to you—that television program you are watching or your children?" your answer would be quick and sure: "My kids." When you are talking with one of your children, but your attention keeps getting drawn to the change of commercials on the tube, it's not that you are revealing your *true* priorities. Rather, you are succumbing to the fact that we can't help but get distracted when distractions arise. For that matter, the whole purpose of television programming (including commercials) is to interrupt our normal lives and grab our attention sound byte by sound byte. Nonetheless, our children are interpreting a different message. They watch our eyes flit back to the screen, they hear us ask, "What did you say?" and they conclude, however mistakenly, that they are not as important to us as that pitchman on the tube trying to sell us a Chrysler Cordoba.

Removing physical distractions not only helps us as listeners but also encourages our children as speakers. They too can be easily distracted and lose their train of thought. If they have

157

something pressing to share, they don't need the added frustration of fits and starts in attempting to communicate it.

Turning down the noise is especially important in specific listening situations. Those times when your daughter comes up to you and says, "Daddy, can we talk?" you need to say, "Sure thing. Here, let me turn off the TV." But turning down the noise also makes good *general* sense. Whatever beneficial value television might have, it remains a noninteractive medium. In other words, it always speaks, never listens, and never encourages its listeners to speak. What it removes from the home is the lively art of conversation. You may be willing to turn off the TV any time your children approach you, but your children may be unwilling to approach you if the TV is on. Quietness encourages conversation.

Turn down the noise by blocking out the demanding voice of your schedule. Active listening requires time. Focused attention means being willing to hear *all* that your children want to say. Have you ever approached someone, only to hear them say, "OK, shoot. But make it short, I have to be somewhere in ten minutes." You begin summarizing whatever it is you wanted to say, but shortly you begin hating yourself for trivializing something that is important to you. Meanwhile, your listener is stealing not-so-inconspicuous glances at his watch. After a while you clam up altogether, knowing that all you are going to get at the end of the conversation is a "Well, that's too bad. I feel for you. Gotta go." And they go, and take your dignity with them.

Active listening that includes the gift of your time communicates love and respect. Generous time also aids you as a listener: You can concentrate on what is being said without darting to thoughts of what you are running late for and what needs to be done. Granted, there are occasions when listening can be quite inopportune. You will need to make decisions between the priority of your child's sudden request for a hearing and the priority of a prior commitment. Those are tough calls. When you do need to leave a conversation before it starts, communicate your love and respect and desire to listen, rather than brushing your child off with, "Tell me some other time, OK?" You can tell your child, "I really want to hear what you have to say. It's so important to me that I want to make sure that you have plenty of time to say what you have to say, and that you get my full undivided attention. That's impossible right now, but let's plan on going out for dessert together after dinner tonight. Just you and I. Can you wait that long? Great. Now don't forget what you're going to tell me. I want to hear it all."

The dynamics of active listening are another argument for the superiority of "quantity time" over "quality time." There are certain times when a child needs to talk or wants to talk. If you are spending a great deal of time with your children, there is a greater likelihood you'll be available when these times arise. Also it is more likely that conversations will occur when a father and child are merely hanging around together. It's difficult to speak from the heart when you are standing in line at Disneyland's Magic Mountain, sharing some quality time.

Turn down the noise by turning a deaf ear to your own prejudged perceptions. The purpose of active listening is to gain understanding. Critical analysis can come later. The wise lecture can follow. For now, simply listen and seek to understand.

There is an important difference between *sympathy* and *empathy*. Sympathy says, "Oh, I feel the same way you do." Empathy says, "I understand how you feel." Occasionally our children will come to us with things that pain us or even anger us. Occasionally what they tell us is so incredibly messed up or so unmistakably wrong that we wonder how this child could ever have come from our loins. Some fathers do not allow their children freedom of expression because they feel that to do so would communicate sympathy or agreement with those wrong thoughts or feelings. But we are not called to sympathy as listeners; we are called to empathy. You don't have to agree with your child's misguided thinking or sin, but you should seek to respect him or her by seeking to understand what he or she is experiencing.

Let patience rule. It's interesting that in the Bible James

159

writes, "Everyone should be *quick to listen,* slow to speak and slow to become angry" (James 1:19, emphasis added). He recognizes that some speeches will make us angry and that containing that anger is important.

The purpose of active listening is to achieve understanding of what your children are thinking and feeling. One of the best ways to be an *active* listener is to ask thoughtful, open-ended questions. Ask questions to gain more information. Ask questions to clarify your understanding. Don't ask questions to engage in cross-examination and to begin building your own case. The goal is empathy. One of the best questions you can ask is "How did that make you feel?"

Turn down the noise by not preparing and practicing your intended speech while your child is talking. You know all those speeches that we fathers have that begin, "When I was your age . . . "? It's important to put those on hold for a moment and let our children tell us what things are like when *they* are their age. Some things about growing up never do change, and you can easily translate your experience and wisdom into the situation. But what is *always* different is that a different human being is experiencing these situations. Your goal as an active listener is to get a handle on the situation and also begin to formulate an opinion of what should be done, but your first goal is to gain an understanding of how your child *perceives* the situation. Since your child is a unique human being, that perception will be different from yours—especially if she's a girl. You need to listen to catch it.

There is a documented tendency among some professional therapists to begin evaluating and dissecting before the client has finished expressing himself.[3] If a father can avoid this trap, he can become empathetic to his children.If you make statements during the crucial parts of a conversation, make "feedback" statements. Feedback statements test whether you are truly understanding what your child is trying to say. Occasionally, interrupt the conversation and say, "OK, let me see if I understand what you mean," then repeat what your child has just told you, but do it in your own words. At that point, your child can say, "No, that's not quite what I mean," and explain further, or she can say, "Yeah, you got it," and proceed with the confidence that she is truly getting through and that you are lovingly listening.

If you fly often, you know that one of the most dangerous types of weather is fog. When fog covers a city and an airport, it can easily shut down that airport for a number of hours. Planes back up and circle overhead. Stranded passengers grumble in the airport lounges. Similarly, America's homes are fogged in with a density of demands and distractions. When a father fails to listen to his children, it can shut down his relationship with them indefinitely. Collisions can occur. But when a father listens, he can get a fix on his children and bring them in for safe landings.

Nine

SECRET 7:
Spiritual
Equipping

In 1988, Cynthia Clark conducted research among families in which the parents were committed to transmitting their religious beliefs to their children. As the focus of her study, she isolated firstborn, early adolescent sons to evaluate how each parent influenced his religious beliefs. Clark found that mothers influenced their sons' practical application of religion—the day-to-day moments where faith touches life. What did the fathers in the study influence? Church attendance.[1] The implication is that fathers focus on their comfort zone—outer religious activity—and neglect, perhaps due to feelings of inadequacy, the practical aspects of a deep, everyday spiritual commitment.

Here is the seventh secret of effective fathers: They understand the spiritual aspects of their children's lives, and they work to help their children discover their own relationship with God.

Spiritual Inadequacy

Actually, it's understandable that many fathers feel inadequate when it comes to spiritual matters. We're surrounded by many other people who seem so much better equipped than we are to foster our children's growth.

There's the pastor. He's had seminary training. He also seems to have the whole Bible memorized. If one of our kids were to come to him with a question, he would reply, "Oh yes, what you are referring to can be found right here," and then he flips to some obscure passage written by some obscure Old Testament prophet, and the text fits the situation perfectly. We thank God for pastors, but they can be intimidating.

There is the youth pastor. We look at our children gathered around him. He's wearing a T-shirt that says, "Jesus is awesome, dude," and he's strumming out chords on his guitar and singing Christian rap music. He seems to have a natural rapport with our kids at the age when our relationship with them tends to be the most strained. And the youth pastor seems to know how to take Jesus Christ and bring him into the issues that we and our children are most concerned about: peer pressure, dating, drugs, etc. We thank God for youth pastors, and they have an important role to fill, but they too can be intimidating.

There are our wives. I don't know how we did it, but many of us ended up married to some very godly women. They are remarkable to watch. They seem to have a natural understanding of spiritual things, an easy camaraderie with Jesus Christ. We watch them pray. We come home and notice that their devotional guide is turned to the right date—they've spent time in the Bible this morning. What's more, they seem to be able to communicate all of this to the children. They sit down with the kids on the couch and read a Bible storybook to them—all about Moses in the bulrushes or Joseph's coat of many colors. (Yes, they can sometimes be intimidating too!)

Typically, women are more relationally driven, while men are more task oriented. This could explain why Christian women seem to have a more natural intimacy with Christ while Christian men seem more drawn to religious duties. God may have blessed us with some very faithful wives, but the temptation that comes with that blessing is to consider our wives too spiritual to

SPIRITUAL EQUIPPING

The effective fathers surveyed showed they felt strongly about teaching Christian values by reading the Bible with their children, having a time of worship in the home, and modeling godly behavior.

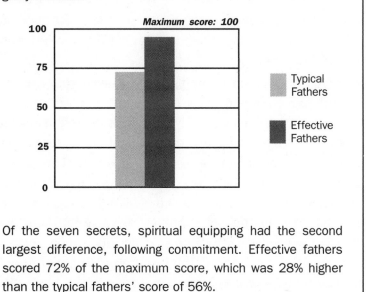

Maximum score: 100

Typical Fathers

Effective Fathers

Of the seven secrets, spiritual equipping had the second largest difference, following commitment. Effective fathers scored 72% of the maximum score, which was 28% higher than the typical fathers' score of 56%.

justify *our* taking the leading role in guiding our family in spiritual matters. After all, isn't the most spiritual person the best choice to equip our children?

It's easy to be intimidated, and easier to delegate spiritual responsibilities to our wives, but we need to embrace our fatherly role as spiritual leaders. Do you have a faithful wife in your home? Do you have a faithful pastor and youth worker in your church? Praise God. Your role as spiritual equipper has been made that much easier. But the presence of these godly people does not make your role unnecessary or any less important. You need to be a part of this team. God has some very significant things for you to contribute.

In dealing with spiritual equipping, we need to address four basic questions:

1. How important is it for my children to be spiritually equipped?

2. How important is it that I, the father, be a spiritual leader?

3. In what ways has God already equipped me as a father to be suitable to the task?

4. In what ways can I prepare myself further to be an effective spiritual equipper?

Actually, I've been assuming that you desire your children to be spiritually equipped. I guess in this age I shouldn't be so quick with my assumptions. Recently, a network TV station in a major midwestern city approached the National Center for Fathering about producing an hour-long prime-time special on fathering. They wanted to use one of our short surveys and asked us for the characteristics that our research had identified regarding satisfied dads. We sent them our findings. Several weeks later, one of their writers called with some specifics about how they were going to format the show. The result was a dramatization for each of the different characteristics that make for a satisfied father. She told us how they were going to dramatize marital interaction and developmental awareness and the other traits. She mentioned them all, except one.

"I'm curious," our staff member said. "How are you going to handle 'spiritual equipping'? You didn't mention that one."

"Oh, we're not going to touch that at all," the writer replied.

"But it's what came out in our research. You'll be presenting an incomplete picture of a satisfied dad without it."

The writer responded, *"Regardless of what the research says,* we can't use 'spiritual equipping.'"

As a researcher, I took a deep breath. As a Christian, I've become used to it. In essence this writer, playing by the rules of our culture, was saying, "I don't care what the truth is, we can't talk about spiritual things."

But the truth of the matter is that there *is* truth. And part of that truth is that there is a God. God exists. He is not like Santa

Claus or the Easter Bunny, about whom we decide whether we want to include them in our family traditions. The question is not *whether* your children will have a relationship with God. The question is *what type* of relationship they will have with him. Your children can be his enemy or his friend. Your children can be his acquaintance or his close companion.

In the same way, part of the truth is that your children are spiritual beings. They possess a spirit—have had one since birth. And that spirit is not like an ear for music or a mechanical aptitude that a child may or may not possess and that you may or may not wish to encourage. Your children can no more decide whether to have a spiritual life than they can decide whether to be a human being. Just as they are developing in their physical and intellectual lives, so they are developing in their spiritual lives. The question is not *whether* your children will develop spiritually. The question is *how well* or *how poorly* this aspect of their lives will be developed.

For too long parents have ignored the spiritual equipping of their children. Today we reap the consequences. Recently *Newsweek* magazine ran a cover story entitled: "Behind the Voter's Revolt: America's Lost Dream." Interestingly, it talked about spiritual needs:

> *Our most profound illusion [as Americans] about prosperity was to think that great doses of it would solve almost any problem. We unwittingly adopted a view of human nature that assumed spiritual needs could ultimately be satisfied with material goods.*[2]

The great motivation for spiritually equipping our children can be found by paraphrasing Mark 8:36 in this manner: "What does it profit a father to teach his children how to gain the whole world, when he fails to teach them how not to forfeit their own souls?"

No Place Like Home

There is a significant historical pattern that established the father as a spiritual leader in the home.

For God's chosen people in Old Testament times, there wasn't a church as we know it. There was a nation, and that nation was made up of tribes, and the tribes were made up of families.

The most important creed among the Hebrews was the *shema*, which is named after the first word of the creed (found in Deut. 6:4-5): "Hear, O Israel: The Lord our God, the Lord is one. Love the Lord your God with all your heart and with all your soul and with all your strength."

The *shema* embodied the greatest truth: that Yahweh was God; the greatest distinctive: that Judaism is monotheistic; and the greatest commandment: that the Israelites were to love God with their total beings. In the presentation of the *shema*, these great truths were followed by God's instructions on how to teach them: "Impress them on your children. Talk about them when you sit at home and when you walk along the road, when you lie down and when you get up" (Deut. 6:7).

God intended his instruction to be part of the day-in-and-day-out routine of family life. The responsibility for introducing the children to the mysteries of the faith fell primarily upon the homes, and only secondarily on the temple, and much later on the synagogue. The manner of instruction seems largely informal: Fathers taught as the opportunity presented itself in the daily walk of life.

With the New Testament, the church emerges. Yet, with whatever changes this brings to the structure of the gathering of God's chosen, the home does not diminish in importance. In all the epistles of the New Testament, which were meant for public reading before the assemblies, children are addressed directly only twice. In both cases (Eph. 6:1 and Col. 3:20), the children are referred *right back* to their parents: "Children, obey your parents in the Lord, for this is right" (Eph. 6:1). The apostle Paul is aware of the responsibility this places on the parents, for he immediately tells parents (fathers in particular) not to exasperate their children, but instead to "bring them up in the training and instruction of the Lord" (Eph. 6:4). The responsibility for spiritually equipping children resides primarily with parents and with the public assembly only secondarily. The apostle Paul illustrates this clearly in 1 Thessalonians 2:11-12: "For you know that we dealt with each of you as a father deals with his own children, encouraging, comforting and urging you to live lives worthy of God, who calls you into his kingdom and glory."

A father certainly needs to be encouraging (speaking words of blessing) and comforting (listening to and understanding concerns) but also urging (helping his children understand the significant role they play in the kingdom of God). This urgency in spiritual matters is vitally important for fathers to express.

Now, the wise father will realize what a valuable asset he has in the local church. He will see it as part of his role as spiritual equipper to expose his children regularly to the teaching found in Sunday school and the discussion and interaction of youth group. Christ has given the members of his church various spiritual gifts, which we use for building one another up in him. The wise father places his son or daughter in the middle of a loving group of gifted people dedicated to using their gifts for the child's benefit. But there is a difference between delegation of responsibility and total abdication. In fact, when a wise father thinks about spiritual gifts, he knows that they are meant "to prepare God's people for works of service" (Eph. 4:12). In other words, he doesn't go up to a teacher in the church and say, "Here's my kid, use your gift to teach him." Instead, he says, "I'm the one called to do the work of service, please equip me so that I can in turn equip my child."

Some writers are quite adamant about this. William Barclay knew the value of parental involvement in shaping the spiritual values of the home. He writes,

171

"The New Testament knows nothing about religious education and nothing about schools, for the New Testament

is certain that the only training which really matters is given within the home, and that there are no teachers so effective for good or evil as parents are."[3]

Barclay may be reflecting the sentiment of the early Puritans. In the 1600s William Gouge relieved some of the temptation of abdicating spiritual equipping to the institutional church by writing that every family is a "little church and a little commonwealth, at least a lively representation thereof, whereby trial may be made for such as are fit for any place of authority or subjection to the church or commonwealth."[4] The well-known writer John Bunyan reveled in the spiritual activity of the home. He was deeply affected by an invitation to the home of a Mr. Gifford, "where I should hear him confer with others about the dealings of God with their souls."[5]

Richard Baxter, a famous Puritan preacher, went so far as to argue for the advantages of instruction in the home as compared to in a larger parish: "(1) there are fewer to teach; (2) the students are always with you and you may speak often; and (3) they are tied to you by relation, affection, and covenant."[6]

Baxter is on the right track. If he were alive today, he might also add that spiritual equipping in the home helps to prevent one of the greatest curses on the modern American church: namely, the compartmentalization of our faith. Children who encounter Christianity only a couple hours out of the week and only within the four walls of a church building will likely grow up to believe that their faith is only one segment of their lives that need not (or cannot) permeate all aspects of their lives. Such children may well make Jesus Lord of their Sunday mornings—while he desires to be Lord of their entire lives. Spiritual equipping in the home allows your children to meet Jesus where they live and in what they do.

In the end, though, we want to avoid the debate that pits the church against the family. Both are God's gifts to your children. The tension between the two, however, can be relentless. When it comes to spiritual equipping, some men favor the church. The central focus of these fathers is on shaping the church to be a productive equipper of their children. In a study of pastors who are fathers, we discovered that these fathers perceived spending time at church as spending time with the family. They had made the assumption that the church *is* the family, and thus when they are at church they are essentially having family time. Their time in the home interacting with their kids was sparse. Then, there are other men who accuse the church of taking away time from their family. They relegate the church to a secondary role, and sometimes do not even become members of a local body of believers. These families are increasing in number and hold the church suspect for its various activities.

But the debate becomes meaningless when each side asks some basic questions. The father asks, How can I be a father in church as well as in the home? How can I use the abounding gifts of the church to help me spiritually equip my children? The church in turn asks, How can we train men to be more effective spiritual equippers in the home?

The Missing Part of the Spiritual Team

Of course, some homes do engage in the spiritual equipping of their children, only it is the mother who does the equipping and the father who watches her in action, often admiringly. But just like the home needs to join the church as a team, so a father needs to join his wife.

Often the father is the missing part of the team. When Dr. Lyle Schaller briefed church leaders, he noted that in a general population of about 53 percent females and 47 percent males, women compose 60 to 62 percent of all Sunday worshipers.[7] Gordon Dalbey quotes this study and notes his own parish experience. In one year, records showed that 63 percent of the active members in his church were women. Among those women who were married, 25 percent worshiped without their husbands. These men either did not join the church or chose not to participate after joining.[8] It led Dalbey to title one of his book chapters "Where Are All the Men?"

But these studies only gauge church attendance. There are plenty of fathers who are active in the church but not spiritually active in their homes. The assumption might be that what the wife does with the children is sufficient for their spiritual growth. This is simply not true. Children need their father's spiritual guidance as well.

There is evidence that spiritual instruction that comes from a father is more likely to "take," or be effective in his child's life, than that coming solely from the mother. For example, one study looked at church attendance among adolescents and adult children. In families where only the mother went to church and took the children with her, a certain percentage of the kids continued to attend church even into adulthood. In families where the father and kids went to church (but the mother did not), a *greater* percentage of the children continued to be regular church attenders. But of course, the greatest percentage of all was found in the children who grew up with *both* parents attending church.

The final conclusion of that study is perhaps the most important. A godly father and mother form a parenting team in which they complement each other to the benefit of the children. What the father brings to the role of spiritual equipper will likely be different than what the mother brings. Children need both. A number of times throughout this book, we've alluded to the phenomenon of the father being the one who usually introduces his children to the world. While the mother is often identified with the home, the father is identified with the outer boundaries of the home. Consequently, when it comes to spiritual equipping, a mother may often be the one to teach the children about the gracious compassion and security of the Lord. Jesus applies a motherly image to himself when he laments over Jerusalem: "How often I have longed to gather your children together, as a hen gathers her chicks under her wings, but you were not willing!" (Luke 13:34). Later, when the apostle Paul applies a fatherly image to himself, he emphasizes a more outward orientation for his children: "For you know that we dealt with each of you as a father deals with his own children, encouraging, comforting and urging you to live lives worthy of God, who calls you into his kingdom and glory" (1 Thess. 2:11-12). The risk for a child who receives spiritual nurturing only from his mother is that the child may grow up to conceive of Christianity as a private affair with no public application. He may limit the exercise of his faith to the four walls of his home and lack the boldness to live for Christ in the workplace.

Of course, for boys who grow up without a masculine model of spiritual vitality in the home, there is the inclination to conceive of Christianity as a feminine pursuit. The workplace has done well in calling men out through specific tasks and rewards for a job well done, but the church has had a tough time in calling men out to live lives of faith. To humbly serve the Lord, love one another, and live pure lives may be equated with being dainty or feminine. What young man would want to embrace that? The feminization of the American church may already be partly responsible for the number of fathers who have abdicated their roles as spiritual equippers in the home. Don't be one of those who succumb to this fear. A proper understanding of who Jesus Christ is and a taste of the courage necessary to live for Christ in this unbelieving world allow for ample expression of a masculine faith. Gordon Dalbey writes:

> *The church has done much over the centuries to encourage men to pursue feminine virtues. But we have not sought and portrayed Christ-centered ways to pursue masculine virtues. It is not enough for Christians to portray weakness and tenderness as acceptable in a man. We also must portray the manly strength and firmness that is of God. We must demonstrate that weakness confessed and submitted to the Living God through Jesus Christ ultimately brings the very masculine strength for which men hunger: toughness in the face of opposition, decisiveness in the face of uncertainty, and saving power in the face of danger.[9]*

175

It is interesting that when the New Testament command is given to bring our children up "in the training and instruction of the Lord," it is not given to mothers (though it certainly applies). It is not even given to parents (though it also applies to the team). *Fathers* are the ones who are singled out in Ephesians 6:4 and Colossians 3:21. The implication is that when the Lord one day inquires about your children, he will ask you, their father, first.

The responsibility may weigh heavily, but God does not give us a task and then fail to give us the resources to complete that task. We need to confront the inadequacy that so many of us feel in our spiritual equipping role.

The effective fathers who comprised our study and who revealed the seventh secret of spiritual equipping are men just like you. They are not seminary grads. They are not missionary retirees. They are not pastors. In fact, while many pastors are also effective dads, our particular sample did not include a single clergyman.

One myth we need to explode is that you have to be a perfect Christian to be an effective spiritual equipper. Hopefully we can all admit that no man is perfect. But we should also avoid the trap that the next best thing to perfection is near perfection. Instead, the next best thing to perfection is honesty. Your honesty and transparency regarding your spiritual life can teach your children much that your near perfection cannot.

William is a friend of mine in ministry who is a real performer. I don't mean that he gets up in the pulpit and playacts or entertains, but rather that he accomplishes much and maintains a positive edge. Yet he may be theatrical in that his positive front is all that he allows others to see, including his children. He has struggled and suffered and learned many deep things from the Lord, but he's never let anyone see him struggling. He told me that he was afraid of weakening the faith of his children by letting them know of these hard times. Lately, though, as William approaches his mid-fifties, he has begun to reflect on some things that he could have done differently. Much of his reflection was sparked by a recent comment by his adult son: "Dad," the son said upon leaving home, "I wish you had told me of your struggles when you were growing up. I mean stuff like sharing your spiritual struggles with me. If you had done that, then I would have known that it is OK to struggle spiritually. Dad, I did struggle spiritually, and I thought I was weird."

Being honest before your children about your own need for God is critical. If you feel inadequate before God, it is only because you are. We all are. "Apart from me you can do nothing," Jesus says (John 15:5). But ironically, confessing your inadequacy makes you adequate in part to the task of spiritually equipping your children. When you are transparent, your young observing children can look inside and see the gracious workings of the Spirit. They will learn much about their own spiritual struggles.

So, don't be ashamed of your sense of inadequacy. But don't be fooled by it either. In our chapter on commitment—the first secret of effective fathers—we said that effective dads draw a great deal of their motivation simply from their *position* as fathers. In other words, while these men might consider themselves *personally* inadequate to the task of fathering, they believe that the role of father itself transfers to them some strength and authority. Even the most mediocre officer can still send the Third Army across the Rhine simply by flashing the five stars on his helmet.

When God commissioned you as a father, he invested in you the power to do his will. In fact, my colleague Dave Simmons comes right out and calls it "father power." He defines it in the following paragraph:

> *God wants His truth and light to pass from one genera-*
> *tion to another so He established an automatic device to*
> *fit into the family to insure His wishes. He created father*
> *power with the strength to span four generations and*
> *inserted it into the hearts of fathers. Father power is like a*
> *tool, a claw hammer, to extract the truth about God out of*

177

one generation and pound it into the next generation, and the third and the fourth.[10]

Dave's reference to a four-generation influence is an allusion to the negative use of father power described in Exodus 34:7: "Yet [God] does not leave the guilty unpunished; he punishes the children and their children for the sin of the fathers to the third and fourth generation."

The point Dave is trying to make is not that it is possible to attain this type of power, but that it is already in your possession, simply because you are a father. *Use your power, and use it for good results.*

When it comes to spiritual equipping, what is the nature of father power? Well, it may reside in the strength of the metaphor: we are fathers like God is a father. We are walking object lessons to our children of who God is.

God created an invisible spiritual universe. But his visible, physical universe is replete with symbols and metaphors that allow us to learn of the spiritual. For example, in marriage we get a chance to experience intimacy and submission. We learn what it means to live as one flesh with another. That's marvelous in itself, but marriage becomes all the more wonderful when we realize that it is a symbol of Christ's love for his church (Eph. 5:22-33).

In the same way, God has an important truth to teach your children: that he is a father. A sense of his fatherliness is crucial to your children's understanding of divine protection, divine provision, divine commitment to us, answer to prayer, etc. God disciplines his followers, but unless your children understand his fatherliness, they will be doomed to perceiving his discipline as cruelty or unforgiving judgment. So God wants to teach each of us about his fatherliness. He does so in the Bible, but he also does so by placing millions of replicas of fatherhood on earth to serve as symbols of his parental care.

God is taking a mighty big risk. Men can just as easily choose to be *bad* models of God's fatherliness, and their children can throw out both model and maker—earthly father and heavenly

Father—in one unfortunate motion. But God knows what he's doing. God realized that ultimately every human model is inadequate in revealing his glory and holiness, so he gave us the Scriptures to describe what kind of father he is. And he still maintains trust in the power of his models. An earthly father can teach a child a lot about the heavenly Father simply by faithfully fulfilling his role as a father.

You have power. Your very presence among your children will affect their spiritual views. You don't even have to open your mouth to fulfill a part of your equipping role. When you stoop down to tie your son's shoe, you are telling him something about God. When you buy your daughter new clothes for school, you are telling her something about God. But the moment you do speak, your voice sounds an awful lot like God's voice to your children. It's not that you *are* God to them, but as far as they know, you sound like him. You are the most important man in the world to them. The simple fact that you *own* a Bible is communicating something valuable to your kids. Of course, owning a Bible but not reading it is also communicating something powerful. You have power as a father. Use it positively.

Don't be paralyzed by a sense of inadequacy caused by comparison to others. Inadequacy becomes a strength when you are honest about it. Inadequacy melts away when you realize the power you have as a father to teach your children spiritual things.

Relax!

Equipping Yourself to Equip Your Children

Working from such a position of strength, you can now ask yourself: In what ways can I equip myself further to be an effective spiritual equipper of my children?

In some ways, the first answer to that question is to grow in your own faith and maturity as a believer in Jesus Christ. Don't be afraid to go up to an older Christian man whom you respect and say, "Fred, I've got an important job to do. I want to be sure

I'm raising my children to follow God. But I can't give them what I don't have. Could you and I get together for coffee once a week? I'd like to have you train me to be a more mature believer." Making such a request of an older man demonstrates that you are seeking to use all the resources God has given you for the sake of your children.

The second answer to the question of equipping ourselves further involves practical tips on how to go about spiritually equipping our kids. Let me offer a few suggestions:

Don't underestimate the power of living a holy life. Spiritual equipping means teaching, but teaching does not necessarily mean preaching. The most effective teaching that a father provides for his son or daughter is his modeling of the truth. The household may be the place for eradicating "little" sins such as lying, cheating, or deceiving, but don't be naive and think you can get away with acting any way you want outside of the home. Guard your integrity. Few things will damage your children more than observing you not practicing what you preach. There has never been such a need in the church and family as there is now for fathers to model this type of spirituality.

One of the most helpful, but frightening, things you can do to promote your effectiveness as a model is to get feedback from your wife and children about your spiritual condition. Ask them point blank if they think your faith is real or fake. These objective yet intimate observers can often give us feedback on things we may never have noticed or thought about.

Lead your family in worship. Perhaps no area of the Christian life has been more neglected by men than worship. In your church, I suspect you have some skilled Bible scholars; you probably have some men who are very effective evangelists, others who have a fruitful prayer life, and still others who have been blessed with a wonderful servant's heart. But how many *worshipers* are there among the men you know? I'm not talking about someone who can conduct a church service by successfully following the program in the church bulletin. Instead, how many men do you know who can freely and comfortably express their adoration and gratitude to the God who is worthy of our praise?

Worship is important. It is important to God. He desires to hear the praise of his people regularly and often. It is important to our families because it can create a sense of solidarity. When we worship together, we experience the bonding of coming together in the Spirit. We also discover our lowest common denominator, something even more basic than our family connections: we discover that God is our Creator and our Father. Worship is also important to men. It can provide a release for males who don't often have the opportunity for emotional expression. When you participate in worship, you focus on someone outside of yourself who can bring a calming effect to all the responsibilities you intuitively feel. This peace exceeds all understanding.

Lead your family in worship through honoring the church service. In Old Testament times, a father had a role in assembling the stones for an altar or preparing a sacrifice. Today the equivalent is in preparing his family for worship on Sunday mornings. The keeping of the Sabbath has been practiced by fathers and families for centuries, at least up until the twentieth century. In our day, it's common for churches to cancel evening services for the Super Bowl or the NBA finals. The Sabbath as a day of rest is being challenged each year by our increasingly commercial society. There is no longer a day of rest, but rather a day to catch up on the things we didn't accomplish during the week.

Now, I'm not proposing that we return to a time of sitting our children on benches in their Sunday best and telling them not to move until the Sabbath sun sets. But we need to convey to our children that our time in church is a very crucial part of the week, set apart for an important purpose, and in this sense holy. When we gather with the saints, we are joining together in a collective voice of praise to our God.

181

The most important leading that you do of your family regarding the Sunday service does not occur during the service itself. Rather, you can do your best work before and after the service. Before the service, make sure that your family is physically, mentally, and spiritually prepared to hear God speak. This may mean something as simple as getting the kids to bed on time (yourself included), so they'll be alert and well behaved at church. Take baths and lay out the children's clothes on Saturday evening, so Sunday morning doesn't become a hectic, aggravating rush. On Sunday morning, put worship tapes on the stereo as your family gets ready. Over a leisurely breakfast, remind everyone that we go to church as participants, not spectators. God is the audience, waiting to hear us sing and pray, delighted in the way we give and listen.

After the service, you have another opportunity to instill respect in your children for the Sunday service. Keep the family together for a little while longer before you head off to the televised football game, your wife drops off to her nap, and your kids take off for the playground. You need to construct a bridge between what you've just experienced within the four walls of the church and how you live your lives in your home and neighborhood. Go out to eat or have a big meal at home. Gathered around the table, you can lead your family in a discussion of the service and sermon. There are some questions you can ask to keep the discussion from becoming more of a critique. You can ask, "What part of the service did you enjoy the most and why?" "What part of the service do you think God enjoyed the most?" "What did you get out of the sermon?" If your kids are young, translate the sermon for them. You'll be surprised at the unique perspectives your kids bring to the discussion, and you may even find *yourself* paying better attention in church next week.

Lead your family in worship at home. I've heard many men express interest in having a regular time when they gather the family together and read the Bible, sing, and pray as a family. Invariably they will ask the question, How do I do it? Family devotions don't have to be a huge or slick production. You also don't need to feel like you have to study and prepare a full-blown sermon for the occasion. In trying to be technique oriented, fathers often forget that they attend a church service once a week and things seem to go pretty well there. With the deluge of published resources—more than fifty different children's Bibles and hundreds of devotional books—having family devotions is not as complex as many fathers make it out to be.

When Jesus was on earth, the disciples came up to him and asked, "Lord, teach us to pray, just as John taught his disciples" (Luke 11:1). We learn to pray by listening to others pray, and we learn to worship by watching others worship. One of the biggest benefits of your family times of worship will be the model they provide for your children. It's fascinating to watch a boisterous young child learn to settle down during prayer as she grows up. Instead of trying to quiet her and exclude her from the family prayer and devotions, let her participate. See what will happen. Give her two or three months to watch and listen, and then encourage her by giving her the opportunity to take part. When the time comes and you gather around the table for prayer, she'll quietly join in.

Use your family devotional times to equip your children with a servant's heart as well. Ask them if they know of anyone among their friends or in the community who could use your family's prayers. Pray for these requests. Keep your ears open to prayer requests, and see if there are ways that God can use your family itself to answer some of them. In fact, brainstorm together: "Mrs. Samuelson is ill; what are some things we can do to help cheer her up?" or "I wonder what we can do to help the Merediths pay their bills?"

Be careful not to equate spiritual equipping with "being in control." Many well-meaning people perceive a father as spiritual if he keeps everyone in his family under tight control. His children never sin (outwardly) because he makes sure they never have the opportunity to do so. Now, obviously a father should not allow chaos to reign in his home, but neither should he have a drill-sergeant mentality, seeking to control his children or put their world under a microscope for *his* detailed inspection. While you may be able to enforce morality for a time,

183

you can never enforce spirituality—which, by definition, is a loving *relationship* with Jesus Christ. Remember, the goal of spiritual equipping is to give our children the spiritual resources they need to live their lives faithfully before God. A legalistic father makes all the choices for his children, and the kids become like a newborn chick who was not allowed to crack its own way out of the shell; it has no strength to survive. As Robert Hicks suggests, "If control is the goal [of fathering], choice must be taken away, and without the freedom of choice, the child can never adequately develop."[11]

Not long ago, the U.S. Senate conducted a serious debate over the issue of prayer in the public schools. Just outside of Washington, D.C., one United States senator who had been involved in the debate went to speak at a church's men's breakfast. In his address, he explained the current debate and then asked those men who were present to raise their hands if they supported prayer in the schools. Almost all the hands in the group went up.

Unexpectedly, he then asked the men another question: "How many of you present today have prayed aloud with your children at home in the last week?" Only two hands went up.

Raising our children to be effective in the Spirit is too important a task to delegate away. Effective fathers rise to the challenge, confident that the heavenly Father will make up for their weaknesses and bless even their most uncertain efforts.

Ten

The Eighth Secret

You are now in possession of the seven secrets of effective fathers. The journeymen have revealed their insights, and now you know about commitment, knowing your child, consistency, protection/provision, loving their mother, active listening, and spiritual equipping. Your apprenticeship enters the phase in which you begin to apply what you have learned. It's time to commit or recommit.

These seven secrets will stand you in good stead, but there is one thing you still lack.

I need to tell you about the eighth secret, believe it or not, the eighth of the seven secrets of effective fathers. Stay with me.

Stretching in all directions from my home here in Kansas lies some of the most fertile farmland in the nation. The farmers here produce grain—mainly wheat. In late June, you can climb a neighboring hill and look down into the valley where the good creek-bottom land is. The fields are like a sea of gold, the wind sweeping through the heads and producing currents and waves of movement. In the distance, a green combine cuts a swath along a field's edge, and the chaff billows out behind the machine in a cloud of dust. The harvest this year is a bumper crop.

What brought about this bounty, this success?

You can talk to these weathered men about successful farming, and they could tell you about soils. They know their ground: the sandy loam, how to terrace it, how to rotate crops. They could tell you about the seed. In Kansas it is Hard Red Winter, an import to America from Russia more than a hundred years ago. These men could tell you about planting seasons, and fertilizer, and herbicide, and irrigation. Some have degrees in agriculture from nearby Kansas State University. Most have inherited generations upon generations of experience on the family farm.

Yeah, but what caused this crop to grow so well? you ask.

"I just told you," the old farmer says. "Good soil, right seed, proper cultivation . . . "

No, what caused this crop to grow at all?

The old farmer stops and pushes the brim of his feed cap up an inch. He takes a long, sweeping view of the endless stretch of land before him and squints at the brilliant reflection of sunlight on his wheat. He thinks he understands. "Do you mean 'what is life?'" he asks.

You are too embarrassed to respond, but that is exactly what you want to know. You've heard plenty about crop rotation and fertilizer choice. You're not even asking about seed germination and photosynthesis. You want to know: What is life? What causes growth?

"I don't know," one farmer says. "It just happens."

"God does it," another one says. "God makes it grow."

A third man volunteers, "It's a mystery, I guess. We do what we know how to do, but you never can tell when a drought's going to come along and ruin us, or when we'll have more rain than we know what to do with. Ultimately it's beyond our control."

As fathers, we have to admit that in truth there is no guarantee that our children will turn out the way we want them to. They are human beings who will make their own choices—and there will be surprises. They'll disappoint us in some ways, and they'll also surprise us by accomplishing things that we never would have thought possible. We hope we've equipped them to handle the trials and temptations that they'll face. We hope we've created an environment in which wise choices are the natural result. But the *choosing* still belongs to our children. That "life" that is in them is something we can influence and shape, but something we can never control. And we will certainly never understand it through scientific means.

In the book *Things We Wish We Had Said,* Tony Campolo writes a letter to his adult son in which he describes his own encounter with the uncertainty of fathering:

> *When we reflect on how Mom and I tried to channel your life, I hope you will think well of us. Undoubtedly, we made mistakes, but we tried hard to do the best we could. In the end, I don't think that parents play the determinative role that they think they do in what their children become. Kids have wills of their own. We parents can provide experiences and training as best we know how, but young people decide for themselves what to do with what parents give them. I think parents take far too much credit when their kids turn out great and far too much blame when their kids mess up their lives. After all, God created two perfect children in Adam and Eve. He placed them in a perfect environment, yet both of them rebelled and did evil. Such can be the consequences of having children with wills of their own. I can only pray that you will continue to will the will of God.*
>
> Love,
> Dad[1]

Fathering is a complex task, perhaps much more than we bargained for when we held our wife in a loving embrace that night and conceived a child. Writing this chapter, I feel much more like a father than I do like a researcher. Between December 1987 and January 1992, the National Center collected data. We used seven different instruments, refined several times. We consulted a host of conceptual analysts, psychologists, statisticians, family data experts, social workers, professors, clergy, and educators. The data was subject to analysis ranging from simple T-tests to Maximum Likelihood Factor Analysis. In the end, though, I remain much like an agronomist from Kansas State, able to tell you about soils that cause good growth, but unable to tell you what the eighth secret is. More variables remain than we as scientists or statisticians can control.

But I can tell you one thing. Actually, I should let farmers tell you. Suppose I approach one of them and ask, "What would you expect to happen at harvest time, if you have done your job faithfully and wisely throughout the year? I mean, if you chose good soil and planted appropriate seed, if you fertilized to the right degree and irrigated if necessary, if you faithfully employed all you know about good farming, what would happen?"

The farmer says, "Then it's likely I'd have a good harvest."

"Even though you don't ultimately know what causes a good crop to grow?"

"Even if I don't know that—no one does," he answers. "I just do my best on my end and hope the rest of it works out all right. Either way, I've done all I can."

"So you can't be absolutely *sure* you'll have a good crop in June?" you ask.

"No, I can't. There are too many things beyond my control," he says. The wise farmer knows that if he is faithful, he can feel confident that he'll reap a plentiful harvest—but he'll also be quick to admit that there are no guarantees.

That opens another set of questions: "What if you decide to do nothing at all? What if you don't plow and disk the soil? What if you don't plant any seed or apply any herbicide or irrigate the fields? What would you expect to happen in June?"

"Oh, then I *know* what would happen," the farmer says with surety. "It'd be like shooting myself in the foot. I'd get nothing, no crop at all."

So it is with fathering. On the one hand, you can do your part by applying the seven secrets of effective fathers, and it is likely you will reap a crop of well-equipped children who live their lives wonderfully before God, though there is no guarantee that this will happen. On the other hand, you can choose to wither in the face of uncertainty and apply none of the principles of fathering that you have learned in this book or from other men or from your own experience. If you opt against faithfully doing what you know you need to do, then you have created your own guarantee in fathering—the guarantee of failure. We all need to apply the seven secrets of effective fathers and humbly allow the rest to remain a mystery.

Mystery and Grace

I have no idea what this eighth secret is. It's a mystery. Flannery O'Connor defines mystery as something which "does not begin except at a depth where adequate motivation and adequate psychology and the various determinations have been exhausted."[2] The apostle Paul uses the word mystery to describe something that "was not made known to men in other generations as it has now been revealed by the Spirit" (Eph. 3:5). So maybe one day we will know many more secrets of effective fathers.

For now, we simply live with the mystery, and it's actually for the best. I am often concerned that our rigorous and spartan scientific perspective on human behavior has allowed the mystery of life to be lost. We simply cannot reduce fathering to a series of foolproof steps leading to instant success. This sort of fathering would be pharisaical and would nullify the inquisitiveness and creativity that each father can bring to the task. So we confess with sincerity that there are some things that we don't know.

If fathering were an exact science, we wouldn't need fathers. In fact, the philosopher Plato proposed that children be removed from their parents immediately upon birth and be raised by state-hired nursemaids. Nice theory. But no society has taken him up on the offer—or no such society has survived. If fathering were an exact science, we could solve the present crisis of fatherlessness in the same manner that we solve, say, chinch bug infestations. Learned people would make a fortune if they could invent a fathering machine.

So the eighth secret is a mystery.

Allowing for the Unknown

Actually, it's possible that each of us possesses this eighth secret. Maybe we just can't verbalize it to each other or even to ourselves. On one of our surveys, we asked the question, "What makes a father successful?" We received one response: "A boat full of gas and the camper hooked up to the trailer." Now, as a researcher you are not allowed to throw out any of the answers you receive, but I was tempted to do so with this one. Some fellow was being humorous or literary, or both.

But the more I thought about his response—"a boat full of gas and the camper hooked up to the trailer"—the more I felt in my gut that this man was serious. For this father, this simple truth may have been a secret that he and his children shared. If he told his answer to one of his adult children, the son would probably smile with a glimmer in his eye, perhaps nod his head, and say, "Yep, Dad, that's what made you so successful as my father." We could try to generalize the response and make some statement about fathers being involved with their kids and sharing common interests, but we would fail to encapsulate the magical mystery of what this experience was for this dad and his kids.

Clair Schnupp is one father who knows what I mean. Clair lives in Ontario, Canada, and has five grown daughters. As they were growing up working on an Indian reservation, he expressed his fathering by helping each of his daughters learn to fly. All five of Clair's daughters have a private pilot's license and can take off and land an airplane. For Clair, this was one secret or shared event that he and his girls had in common. But would you advise all fathers to go out and take flying lessons? No. There's a mystery in that. The mystery of Clair Schnupp the father and his five sweet daughters. The mystery of a boat full of gas and a camper hooked up to the trailer.

I suppose one secret I learned from my father was eating ice cream. What that has to do with fathering, I don't know. But it was one event that my father enjoyed sharing with his children. Each one of us kids knew full well that he would go for a drive during the summer and would purposely drive by the Dairy Queen until one of us begged him to stop for an ice cream cone. Inevitably, he would pull in and satisfy his children's desires as well as his own.

There was something good about our little summer ritual. It has to do with fathering and growing up and being a family, but I can't explain it. It's a mystery.

When it comes to fathering, there is a secret within each father that he longs to express with his kids, and it normally allows for some shared memories to develop between a father and child. This secret may be the most profound of them all. It is each man's individual expression of his fathering.

If we have each been given this eighth secret of effective fathering, then that means that the secret—like the mystery of life itself—ultimately resides within the heart of the God who created us. He knows what he's doing. It's no accident that we have the children we have. The Bible says, "Children are a gift of the Lord" (Psalm 127:3, NASB). In his sovereignty, that also means that our *particular* children—we can name them by name—are also gifts of the Lord. He did not give us the wrong kids, nor did he give them to the wrong man. That means that *you* are the only person whom he intends to father *your* children. Other men may *stepfather* your children, the schools may nurture your children, your wife may mother your children, and the government may foster your children, but only *you* can *father* your children. *You* are the only one in possession of that secret that God wants implemented in the lives of your children.

We give ourselves to the grace of God. We do what we know he wants us to do, and we trust him for the rest. We become devoted fathers who live by faith.

The Eighth Wonder

Seven secrets. Seven tasks. Seven wonders of the world.

Not long ago, I had the opportunity to speak to forty elementary students about the important role of the father. As I began my discussion, I asked if any of them had been to the Taj Mahal or the ruins of Ephesus. None had. As I explained the seven wonders of the ancient world, they all seemed uninterested until I told them that they might have an opportunity to visit the eighth wonder of the world.

I began to describe the preparation that it takes to visit this eighth wonder. "It will cost you a lot of money, time, and sleep," I said, "but to see it is simply magnificent." In fact, the grandeur of this wonder makes the Great Pyramids of Egypt, and the Hanging Gardens of Babylon pale in comparison. It takes about nine months of preparation, but then when the time is ripe you can leave and get ready for the adventure. Your bags are packed, and you head to the local hospital and wait patiently for this wonder to arrive. There is a sense of nervousness and sickness that accompanies the wait. But then the time arrives. When the baby is born and you see his first breath change the color of his face, then you know you have seen the eighth wonder of the world.

Eight wonders. Eight secrets.

A God of grace.

Appendix A

About
the
Research

Few would disagree with the premise that fathers need both resources and helps to optimize their relationship with their children. Resources are often developed after investigation. Thus the need to develop a respectable data base is vital. With new data and increased attention to fathering research, practitioners are able to shape resources to aid fathers.

Beginning in 1987, research on the role and function of fathers began to take shape through what is now called the National Center for Fathering. An immediate literature review was undertaken with sources dating beyond B.C. 200. Not only did we examine the 1190-plus biblical references to fathers, fathering, and fatherlessness, but we reviewed other pertinent Greek and Egyptian literature. Plutarch's *A Precedent to Parents* and Xenophon's *Treatise of the Household* were among works still being printed into the sixteenth century. Their influence cannot be understated. Whitford's *A Work for Householders* enjoyed six editions in the fourteenth century. Later Gouge's *Of Domestical Duties* was a popular book aimed at heads of households in England, while Mather's *Pray for the Rising Generation* was read by American Puritan fathers.

197

The aforementioned works are far from an exhaustive list of the literature that was reviewed. The historical existence of this literature illustrates the need to consult the body of material that has existed for centuries. These historical works were then combined with more than four thousand journal articles, dissertations, abstracts, and books that have been generated about fathering in the last forty years.

After a thorough literature review was completed, leading family data professionals and experts discussed the development of an instrument to identify fathering strengths and weaknesses. The initial instrument sought to identify twenty-seven aspects related to fathering that the literature and experts in the field had identified as important. Walter Schumm, Ph.D., Robert Buckler, M.D., Judson Swihart, Ph.D., George Rekers, Ph.D., Carrol E. Kennedy, Ed.D., Suzan Hawkes, M.S.W., Gary Klozenbucher, M.S.W., Gale Roid, Ph.D., and the author reviewed both the theory and the development of the "Fathering Styles Inventory," which gave rise to the Personal Fathering Profile (PFP).

Following an initial data collection (N=2066), six subsequent samples (N=3044) have been collected in order to increase diversity within the overall data base and strengthen the reliability of the PFP. Efforts have been made to include all types and persuasions of fathers: minority, incarcerated, military, step, noncustodial, and cross-cultural fathers. Field specialists were also consulted. Emerson Eggerichs, Ph.D., David A. Simmons, D.Min., Paul Lewis, Charles T. Aycock, and Paul Heidebrecht had some input on the development and initial data collection.

Currently more than four thousand fathers have provided data from their own experiences for analysis. This material has been collected through interviews, responses to open-ended questions, and scales developed to assess a father's fathering. The report of much of the statistical data can be found in social science publications, e.g., *Psychological Reports,* etc.

Ongoing research is currently being conducted to study other issues vital to fathering. These issues include religiosity, life-cycle influences, fathering in minority settings, incarcerated fathers, military fathers, etc. A national random sampling will be completed in 1992. The results of these findings will be published in scientific publications and in general interest books such as this one. The National Center for Fathering also hosts an annual national conference committed to networking with other leaders and advocates of fathers.

The Jennifer Capriati Story

Ever since her father started grooming her for tennis at age five, Jennifer Capriati has made all her competitors look, well, like children. When she burst onto the professional scene at age fourteen, Capriati was hailed as the future of women's tennis. She signed a $6 million endorsement contract before her first match. She has reached the quarterfinals or semifinals in four or five grand slam tournaments and was ranked sixth in the world at age fifteen.

Her father, Stefano, manages her career. During these last two years, he has pushed and pushed her, setting her up for tournaments and high-paying exhibitions all over the world, challenging the limit on the number of appearances a player can make before her sixteenth birthday. He has taken her away from the normal social events that teenagers want to experience; he has denied her her adolescence in favor of lucrative endorsements and the pursuit of number one.

In January of this year, after Jennifer lost to a top seed in the Australian Open, she fell apart, burst into tears, and told a reporter that she thought everyone hated her when she lost. But instead of flying home to be with her friends, Jennifer was whisked off to Hong Kong for an exhibition, and then to Japan, where she lost to a player ranked far below her, 6-1, 6-2.

Some people believe she sees herself as a failure because Stefano has set her up to think losing always means failure, and now she has quit trying because she just wants to go home, which is reasonable for a fifteen-year-old girl. The sports world seems somewhat ashamed. Stefano Capriati wanted fame for his daughter and perhaps millions for his

199

family. Now what he has is a burned-out, exasperated teenage child.

Formula fathers like this kill the goose to get to the golden eggs—the results—and too often end up with "goose eggs," that is, with nothing.

Fortunately, it appears as though Stefano Capriati is learning from what has happened. He has recently backed off from controlling his daughter's career by enlisting a professional tennis coach and a personal manager. Now he can focus on his role as a father, where Jennifer is no longer a millionaire tennis superstar, but just a teenage girl who needs lots of patience and understanding.

From a radio transcript, John Feinstein, National Public Radio's "Morning Edition" (February 6, 1992).

Appendix B

Fatherlessness: A National Epidemic

In our country today, 5.6 million children under the age of fifteen are growing up without fathers.[1] *Daddy's not home.* Maybe he was a teenager himself who stayed around long enough to get his teenage girlfriend pregnant. Now, when this mother talks about him to her children, or anyone else, it's with a sad look in her eye and a curse on her lips. Maybe Dad's divorced from Mom, and the kids see him on weekends. Or the company has moved him to the coast, so her kids have a father only a couple of times a year. One study has shown that no matter how amicable the divorce settlement might have been, two years later the average divorced dad has little or no contact with his children. It's staggering to think that three-fourths of all children of divorce have contact with their fathers fewer than two days a month.[2]

Or maybe there was no divorce. Maybe one day at the dinner table Dad simply stood up and announced to his wife and kids, "I'm leaving." And then he did. And there's a little child—5.6 million of them actually—who stands at the window, wipes the steam off the glass, and stares out into the rain, watching for Dad to come home.

Of course, there's more than one way for a father to be absent, more than one way for a child to be fatherless. That figure of over 5 million children does not include those whose fathers are emotionally or mentally absent (*distant*, we say), which would surely add several million more. Maybe they're so engrossed in their jobs and the other pressures they face every day that they don't have time to be involved in the lives of their children. It could be they've never realized what a positive force they can be in their children's lives. Or maybe they've never been around kids enough to be comfortable relating to them.

What I am sure of is that fatherlessness is a crisis. In January 1992, Health and Human Services Secretary Louis W. Sullivan called it "the greatest family challenge of our era."[3] The previous year, on Father's Day, an editorial by Secretary Sullivan appeared in newspapers across America. He told us not to be fooled; this crisis crosses barriers of race and class to touch each one of us. Concerning the issue of unwed pregnancy, for example, 63 percent of black births in 1988 were to unmarried mothers. To think that we are witnessing a major American community moving toward almost total fatherlessness! Equally astounding is the trend among unmarried *white* teens, who accounted for a substantial 81 percent of the increase in unwed teen births.[4]

Perhaps we could measure the effects of fatherlessness in financial terms. Again with the issue of unwed pregnancy, unmarried teen births have cost the public an estimated $22 billion.[5] A youth worker among gangs in Los Angeles has told me that the common denominator among these gang members is their fatherless homes. In fact, that's the attraction of the gangs: "They provide the commitment and protection that is missing from their lack of a father."[6] One columnist in the *Washington Post* argues that "in the midst of our current domestic chaos, fatherhood is an effective, no-cost law-enforcement and social-work program."[7]

204

The psychological impact of fatherlessness upon children is staggering. Studies show that children who grow up in fatherless homes are more likely to:

- drop out of high school
- suffer from poverty
- receive welfare
- marry early
- have children out of wedlock
- divorce
- commit delinquent acts
- engage in drug and alcohol use[8]

There is another measure of the damage of fatherlessness, one with which you may identify immediately. You see, it's actually impossible for a father to be truly absent; part of him is always there. But in the fatherless home, he has given up his right to represent himself, and he often gets translated into a ghost, or a haunting spirit, or some would say a demon. No statistic can adequately measure the amount of pain caused by an absent father.

Research tells us that a father influences his children in many ways. Most notably a father exerts influence on the following:

- the intellectual ability of his children
- the behavior his children will model
- the genetic background that his children receive
- his children's ethnic heritage and their position in the family structure
- the occupational choices his children make
- the material resources his children are left with when he is gone
- the ways his children will behave toward their offspring
- the attitudes his children will hold regarding their children
- the memories his children will have after he dies or separates from the family[9, 10]

What a powerful potential we fathers have in the lives of our children!

There is a host of scientific studies that document the critical

205

role of fathering. There is, however, a dark side to this. These consequences of fatherless households are like a fire that is burning in our culture. This fire has destroyed human life and property and has desecrated what was once beautiful scenery. At the focal point of this fire are the embittered feelings and the wanton neglect of our most precious resource, our children. We have all been children, and we know the intensity of this blaze, not to mention the potential it holds for further disaster.

Henri Nouwen accurately predicted this blaze twenty years ago when he said that this present generation would be a generation without fathers, a society of fatherlessness. Nouwen, a Catholic priest, looked intently into the eyes of the youth and foresaw the coming inferno.[11] I wish Nouwen had been wrong, but this burning fire in our culture continues to leave many homeless. We need fathers first and men second to put out the fires of fatherlessness. *You* are critical to this task.

The potential power in our fathering roles is, for most of us, *more power than we'll ever possess in any other area of our life.* It's scary, but it's also thrilling. It's immensely satisfying when we wield that power wisely, as heroes who fight for the futures of their children, but it can also be so destructive: the effects of fatherlessness can torment a man *and* his children for the rest of their lives.

You and I will likely never be in the White House for anything more than a tour. We may not be finding new cures in the medical research lab. But you and I are raising the parents and leaders of the twenty-first century, and we believe that they have the potential to accomplish what we can only dream of. The encouragement, the teaching, the discipline, and the affection we give our children will be bearing fruit long after we're dead—quite possibly even long after our children and children's children are gone.

For good or evil, we are literally shaping the future.

The future is your children. The choice is yours.

Appendix C

The National Center for Fathering

The National Center for Fathering can make available to you the same survey that we gave to the four thousand men of our research database. When you mail our 168-item questionnaire in to our offices, we return to you a twelve-page, computer-generated report that will give you feedback on how you are doing with the seven secrets and more. More important, we provide you with curriculum material that can help you lead a fathering small group of your own.

For more information on how to purchase the Personal Fathering Profile and fathering group curriculum, please call or write to:

The National Center for Fathering
P.O. Box 1918
Manhattan, KS 66502
(913) 776-4114

The Mike Harper Story

My name is Mike Harper. I was born on November 12, 1967, in Anderson, Indiana. I was a healthy baby, not any different than most infants. What was unusual was the fact that the woman who gave birth to me was only a child herself. My mother was only fifteen. She was a child having a child.

There was another thing unusual about this situation. My mother's parents were there as well as her older sister, but where was my father? Of course there was a man who would later be married to my mother, but he was not my father.

So here is my mother at the age of fifteen, having a baby without the support or help of the man who helped conceive me. Being a child, she was not ready to become a mother. She did give motherhood a shot though.

My mother eventually married the man who was with her at my birth, but this relationship didn't work out, and they were divorced. Their marriage had only lasted a short time. At her age she was not responsible enough to be a mother, a wife, and her own person.

My future and my care were a great concern of my grandparents. They offered to adopt me from their daughter. My mother agreed, and so from the age of three I was raised by my grandparents. This was a chance for my mother to grow up and become a more responsible person, and it allowed me to have better care and a more stable environment and future.

These facts of the adoption and who my mother was were never hidden from me. I grew up knowing and visiting my mother during the summer. Growing up with my grandparents was very rewarding, but it was a different situation than other children had. I knew my grandparents were much older than other children's parents. They just could not be involved as much as other parents because of their age. When I would receive information cards in school, I would often be confused by the very first line. It would ask "Father's name." Although I knew to put my grandfather's name, I often reflected on the question, "Who is my real father?"

I became more involved with extracurricular activities in

middle school. I wanted the support of my grandparents, especially my grandfather, at my athletic activities. Although they supported me as much as possible, this made me question who my father was even more.

During my eighth-grade year, my grandmother became ill and passed away. This was very hard on all of us. This experience catapulted my grandfather and me into a one-on-one relationship. We were to spend the next four years living together as just two men taking care of themselves and each other. I had no choice but to really get to know the man who had been my "father" since the age of three.

As my grandfather and I grew together, I began to realize even more what his qualities were, and I admired him for them. He was a very stern man and would not hesitate to discipline a grandchild. Through all his stubbornness I could see his love and the joy he had. He was a teddy bear inside and was very much a wise guy being very witty. He could always make me laugh.

My mother had decided to return home for financial reasons. She had lived in Las Vegas, where she got into financial problems due to drug use. She ended up running away from it. Since the time I had been adopted, she had been involved in more than one interracial relationship, from which she had two more children. That was kind of hard for most of my immediate family to swallow, but it really made little difference to me.

The relationship with my grandfather and the return of my mother to our hometown caused me to consider my past more important. But, I never pursued the area, thinking maybe there was something I should not know or would be told sooner or later. Sure enough, on my fifteenth birthday I was told about my natural father. We visited my grandmother's grave, and my mother took me to my father's grave.

Most of the story unfolded that day, with smaller pieces being put in since then. As it fits together, my father was a boy my mother met at church. They became involved but never took responsibility as a couple for me. They eventually went their separate ways. My father's way took him to Vietnam,

211

where he became addicted to drugs. He returned home, married, and eventually had three children. He still could not break the drug habit. This habit brought him to robbing a store, and in the process he was shot and killed.

I was so relieved to know the truth about my father. I finally knew who he was and what he was and how he was. Although I was much relieved to know all this, I still did not have a father like everyone else. I felt let down and discouraged because I would not have a father.

Life went on, and I developed good friendships my junior and senior years in high school. I became involved with friends that had high morals and dared to be different than all the others who just could not wait for a party. I also became involved with a girl who was a pastor's daughter. Her family was a tremendous example of what a family should be like. I clung to them and became very close.

My involvement with my friends showed me the way I wanted to act. Two friends of mine were a little different. I came to know them as Christians. I never thought deeply about this because I thought I was a good guy. I was fine with my situation. I later came to find out my girlfriend was a Christian, and she wanted me to come to know God personally. I was very closed-minded to the idea and rejected it totally. Our relationship continued, but it was never quite the same.

All this time I was becoming more of an independent person. I did not spend as much time with my family and grandfather. My grandfather became sick my senior year and was diagnosed with cancer. I was very shocked and did not know what to expect. His illness lasted three months. It totally destroyed this man of such strong stature. It reduced him to someone who needed twenty-four-hour care. The family took care of him during this time. I really did not want to deal with the hardship, so I didn't offer much help. The man I knew as my father my whole life was soon to die.

I spent the last week of his life at home with him trying to think what more I could do for him. He had given me so much, and now he was not going to let me give anything back to him.

His death was the worst time in my life. I no longer had a father. I was very much alone. I began to ask myself What am I going to do with my life? and What is going to happen when I die?

This progressed through my freshman year in college. I eventually broke up with my girlfriend from high school, but I became closer to another one of my Christian friends from high school. I got to see his life every day. He relied on God daily and had a way to deal with anxieties and pressures. Most of all he had someone to talk to and be with spiritually. He knew where he was going. I desired to have those same feelings and confidence. I was eventually presented with the gospel in a clear and concise manner. I found out that God accepts me as I am. He would mold me and change me. He would raise me as an adopted son.

I immediately desired to know more about him. I began reading the Bible and praying. My two Christian friends were a great encouragement. I have been like a child and fallen down a few times, but God has been there to pick me up.

God has shown me his aspects as a father. He has been a provider since his plan for me took shape by letting my grandparents adopt me. If I had been with my mother, I am sure I would hot have been able to attend college and pursue my education. Because God allowed me that opportunity, I now have a more secure future.

I have been blessed to be associated with Campus Crusade for Christ. I have developed my relationship with God dramatically through this organization. I have been able to be discipled by a staff member, and I have attended numerous conferences for training and fellowship with other college students.

The one quality I have most admired and clung to is the love of God. As I study that God is love, I see more how God wants us to know that love, above all else! His love is infinite and eternal toward those who know him. He desires for us to come into a close relationship with him. To look back on my life is to look at the love God has shown me. Out of all the people in my family, he picked me to represent him. He has left me with a unique situation where I can look only to him as a father. He has woven a perfect plan for my life and kept me from only he knows what. His love was ever before him as he continued reaching out to me when I did not know him. Since I have come to know him, he has given me a purpose. He has given me the chance to help change people's lives by introducing them to their heavenly Father. When people face the same or similar situations, I can point them to a Father whom King David relied upon in Psalm 89:26: "You are my Father, my God, the Rock my Savior."

Notes

Chapter 1. The Voices of Effective Fathers

1. Sara McLanahan and Karen Booth, "Mother-Only Families: Problems, Prospects, and Politics," *Journal of Marriage and the Family* 51 (1989): 557-580.

2. *The American Family Under Siege* (Family Research Council, 1989), 1.

3. Bud Greenspan, "The Greater Part of Glory," *Parade Magazine, 21 April 1991, 5.*

Chapter 2. Applying the Seven Secrets

1. Emerson E. Eggerichs, Jr., *A Descriptive Analysis of Strong Evangelical Fathers* (1992). Unpublished doctoral dissertation, Michigan State University, East Lansing, Michigan.

2. Dallas Willard, *Spirit of the Disciplines* (San Francisco: Harper, 1988), 138.

3. Pete Rose, "SuperJock Pete Rose Talks about Women, Divorce, and Fatherhood," *MS* (June 1983), 68.

Chapter 3. Secret 1: Commitment

1. Christopher DeVinck, *The Power of the Powerless* (New York: Doubleday, 1983), 13.

2. Michael Lamb, *Fathers and their Families* (Hillsdale, N.J.: Analytic Press, 1989), 16.

3. Bonnie Blair, interview, CBS Sports (February 10, 1992).

4. Arman M. Nicholi, George Rekers, ed., *Family Building* (Ventura, California: Regal Books, 1985), 52.

5. *Ibid.*

6. Nicky Marone, *How to Father a Successful Daughter,* (New York: Ballentine Books, 1988), 65.

7. Ted Engstrom, *The Pursuit of Excellence* (Grand Rapids: Zondervan Publishing, 1982), 52.

8. Martin Greenberg, M.D., *The Birth of a Father* (New York: Continuum, 1985), 18.

Chapter 4. Secret 2: Knowing Your Child

1. William Whatley, *A Bride-Bush or a Direction for Married Persons* (London: STC25299, 1619), 15.

2. Josh McDowell and Dr. Norm Wakefield, *The Dad Difference* (San Bernardino: Here's Life Publishers, 1989), 12.

3. Bernie May, "Learning to Scan," *In Other Words* (Huntington Beach: Wycliffe, 16:3), 8.

Chapter 5. Secret 3: Consistency

1. Erma Bombeck, *Family—The Ties that Bind . . . and Gag!* (New York: McGraw-Hill, 1987), 2.

2. Gordon Dalbey, Healing the Masculine Soul Seminar, Manhattan, KS, March 23, 1991.

3. The Talmud, Sukkah 46B.

4. Sue Schellenbarger, "Men Find More Ways to Spend Time at Home," *The Wall Street Journal*, 12 February 1992, B1.

Chapter 6. Secret 4: Protecting and Providing

1. Richard Llewellyn, *How Green Was My Valley* (New York: Macmillan, 1940), 2-3.

2. Ruth Calkin, *Lord, It Keeps Happening and Happening* (Wheaton, Ill.: Tyndale House Publishers, 1984), 84.

3. Glen Elder, *Children of the Great Depression* (Chicago: University of Chicago Press, 1974), 291

4. Charles A. Corr and Joan N. McNeil, *Adolescence and Death* (New York: Springer Publishing Co., 1986), 138.

5. John A. McAdoo, "Black Perspective on the Father's Role in Child Development," *Marriage and Family Review* 9:4 (1987): 117-133.

6. Vonnie McLoyd, "Socialization and Development in a Changing Economy," *American Psychologist* 44 (1989): 293-302.

Chapter 7. Secret 5: Loving Their Mother

1. Family Research Council, *The American Family Under Siege* (Washington, D.C.: U.S. Government Printing Office, 1989).

2. U.S. Bureau of the Census, *Statistical Abstracts of the United States: 1950-1988* (Washington D.C.: U.S. Government Printing Office, 1950-1988).

3. Asa Baber, "Decade of the Dad," *Playboy* (January 1990), 33.

4. Judith Wallerstein, *Second Chances* (New York: Ticknor and Fields, 1989), 297-300.

5. Sara McLanahan and Karen Booth, "Mother-Only Families: Problems, Prospects, and Politics," *Journal of Marriage and the Family* 51 (1989) 557-580.

6. Gene Brody, "Marital Quality and Mother-Child and Father-Child Interactions with School-Aged Children," *Developmental Psychology* 22 (1986): 291-296.

7. W.D. Erickson, "The Life Histories and Psychological Profiles of 59 Incestuous Stepfathers," *Bulletin of the American Academy of Psychiatry and the Law* 15 (1987): 349-357.

8. Shill Levy, "Antecedents of Fathering: Some Further Exploration," *Developmental Psychology* 24 (1988): 434-440.

9. Bette Runch, "Families in Hard Times: A Legacy," *Families Today* (Washington: Department of HEW, 1979), 49.

10. William Whatley, *A Bride-Bush or a Direction for Married Persons* (London: STC25299, 1619), 15.

11. Lee Horton, "The Father's Role in Behavioral Parent Training: A Review," *Journal of Clinical Child Psychology* 13 (1984): 274-279.

Chapter 8. Secret 6: Active Listening

1. Paul Tournier, *To Understand Each Other* (Atlanta: John Knox Press, 1967), 8. Quoted in *What Kids Need Most in a Dad* by Tim Hansel (Old Tappan, NJ: Fleming H. Revell, 1984), 167

2. Ross Campbell, *How to Really Love your Child* (Wheaton, Illinois: Victor Books, 1979), 56.

3. Gerard Egan, *The Skilled Helper* (Belmont, Calif.: Brooks/Cole, 1986), 73-93.

Chapter 9. Secret 7: Spiritual Equipping

1. Cynthia Clark, "The Transmission of Religious Beliefs and Practices for Parents to Firstborn Early Adolescent Sons," *Journal of Marriage and the Family* 50 (May 1988): 463-72.

2. Robert J. Samuelson, "How Our American Dream Unraveled," *Newsweek* (March 2, 1992), 38.

3. Dean Merrill, *Together At Home* (Nashville: Thomas Nelson, 1985), 194.

4. William Gouge, *Of Domesticall Duties* (London: STC12119, 1622), 18.

5. John Bunyan, *Grace Abounding to the Chief of Sinners* (London: Allen & Urwin, 1907), 50.

6. Richard Baxter, *Practical Works* (1673: 4:231).

7. Gordon Dalbey, *Healing the Masculine Soul* (Dallas: Word, 1988), 174-175.

8. *Ibid.*, 175.

9. *Ibid.*, 180.

10. Dave Simmons, *Dad the Family Coach* (Wheaton, IL: Victor Books, 1991), 40.

11. Robert Hicks, *Uneasy Manhood* (Nashville: Thomas Nelson, 1991), 134.

Chapter 10. The Eighth Secret

1. Tony and Bart Campolo, *Things We Wish We Had Said* (Dallas: Word, 1989), 37.

2. Flannery O'Connor, Sally and Robert Fitzgerald, eds., *Mystery and Manners* (New York: Farrar, Strauss, Giroux, 1961), 4.

Appendix B. Fatherlessness: A National Epidemic

1. Pat Wingert and Patricia King, "And What of Deadbeat Dads?" *Newsweek*, 19 December 1988, 66.

2. Louis W. Sullivan, "Absentee Fathers Tarnish Tradition of Father's Day," *The Allen American*, 16 June 1991, A9.

3. "Report Calls Lack of Fathers' Greatest Family Challenge," *The Orange County Register*, 10 January 1992, A7.

4. Sullivan, 1991.

5. Sullivan, 1991.

6. Wayne Perriman, speech titled "Gangs: Counterfeit Families and Fathers," April 13, 1991.

7. Jack Kammer, "Winning Votes by Saying Some Good Things about Fathers." *Washington Post*, 21 September 1991.

8. Sara McLanahan and Karen Booth, "Mother-Only Families: Problems, Prospects, and Politics," *Journal of Marriage and the Family* 51 (1989): 557-580.

9. Marshall L. Hamilton, *Fathers' Influence on Children* (Chicago, Ill., 1977).

10. Nelson Hall, A.J. Hawkins, and J. Belsky, "The Role of the Father Involvement in Personality Change in Men across the Transition to Parenthood," *Family Relations* 38 (1989), 378.

11. Henri J.M. Nouwen, *The Wounded Healer* (New York: Doubleday, 1972), 27.

A Guide for Group Study

The following guide has been designed for use in small-group settings. The questions correspond to the content in each chapter. I trust that they will be helpful as you consider the tremendous opportunity you have in shaping the leaders of the future generations.

Session One: The Voice of Effective Fathers

This session focuses on the importance of fathers. Draw from your own childhood experience and seek to understand why you father the way you do.

---

1. As you think about your role as a father, identify two men whom you respect for their commitment to fathering. What specifically do you respect in them?

---

2. Who has prepared you most for the task of fathering?

---

3. What priority do you give fathering among the other important roles you fulfill? What do you use to justify these priorities?

4. Do you agree with the statement that fathering needs to be learned? If so, how do you learn more about becoming a better father?

5. What hopes do you have for your children? What type of people do you want them to grow up to be? Be specific if you can.

Session Two: Applying the Seven Secrets

A baseball player may change his batting style from time to time; a young writer seeks to develop an effective writing style. These can be very technical, tangible adjustments, often with help from coaches and teachers. In the same way, there are practical and productive ways we can improve at fathering when we are willing to enlist help from others and do the work that's necessary.

1. Which two passages of scripture have given you the most encouragement as a father?

2. People have financial plans to review their net worth over the years. Or someone may have a savings plan or a budget plan. Why not have a fathering plan? What type of plan do you have for strengthening your fathering? What would such a plan look like? What resources might you use to develop a fathering plan?

3. If your children were able to give you feedback as a father, in what area would they encourage you to improve?

4. How do you think the principle of accountability relates to the role of fathering? Is it important?

5. To whom are you accountable for your fathering? Who holds your feet to the fire in training your kids?

Session Three: Commitment

Under oath, we would all say that our children are important to us, but with fathering, true commitment takes feelings and makes actions out of them; it makes *declared* priorities into visible, *life-style* priorities.

1. Who is the most committed father you know? What impresses you about his commitment to fathering?

2. Did your father ever tell you that he was committed to you? How did he express his commitment? How did it make you feel?

3. When did you determine that you were going to be a committed father? What led you to that particular point?

4. Describe how TV, the public school system, and the federal government are each actively fathering children in America.

5. Who are some other father figures that affect your fathering (e.g.: an elder in your church, an uncle, etc.)?

6. What are some of the ways that you express your commitment daily to your children?

Session Four: Knowing Your Child

Do you ever feel like the things you're trying to do for your kids are backfiring, and it seems like you're never really hitting it off? Knowing your child will influence your actions, so you—and your kids—can get the most out of your efforts.

---

1. Where did you learn the most about child rearing? What are some of your resources for information and advice?

---

2. What, specifically, makes your child different from other children of the same age?

---

3. What gifts or talents does your child have that are different from yours?

4. What are ways that you can "proactively" learn more about your kids?

5. Make a list of the major issues in which you need to be directly involved when it comes to making sure your kids are aware (e.g.: drugs, finances, politics, etc.).

6. What are some indicators that suggest your child may be struggling with drugs or being sexually active?

7. What are some situations that an intrusive father would likely butt into where he really has no business involving himself?

Session Five: Consistency

Every young "mapmaker" needs an environment of stability. Our children need us to be regular and predictable in our person, our actions, and our habits.

---

1. List some of the areas in which your children look to you for consistency.

---

2. Consistency is synonymous with trust. How can your becoming consistent strengthen your children's trust in you?

---

3. What are three things your father did consistently with you over the years? What is one thing you wished he would have *become* consistent in?

4. How do you perceive God as a consistent father? What, specifically, does he do to demonstrate his consistency?

5. If a father is divorced and does not have custody of his children, how can he display consistent actions toward his children? What are some practical things he can do?

Session Six: Protecting and Providing

God knew what he was doing when he made us to be men, and one of the gifts he has given us is the need and the ability to protect and provide for our family. Your feelings about being a man are basic to being an effective protector and provider.

1. The way your great-grandfather provided for and protected his family was different from what fathers do today. In what ways do you need to provide for and protect your family that your great-grandfather didn't? What did your great-grandfather need to do that you don't?

233

2. What is or was the toughest crisis you have had to face as a father? What helped you through it?

3. Growing up, what crisis did you see your father or mother endure? What sticks out in your mind as you review that experience?

4. How does your role of being a financial provider relate to your feelings of satisfaction as a father?

Session Seven: Loving Their Mother

Some scholars and psychologists have devoted their entire life to studying the marriage relationship. Obviously, one chapter cannot cover it completely, but we should at least appreciate the great significance a strong marriage can have for your kids.

---

1. What word picture best describes your relationship with your wife?

---

2. In what ways have you observed your marital relationship affecting your children?

---

3. When you've seen a husband and wife work together as a team to understand their children, what positive results have you observed?

4. What insights have you gained from your wife that have helped you strengthen your relationship with your children?

5. What are some of the effects of divorce you've observed in children?

6. How would your children describe your relationship to their mother?

7. When was the last time you had an opportunity to be with your wife alone, without the kids, for more than twelve hours?

Session Eight: Active Listening

Active listening is to our fathering what the Bible is to our spiritual life—it gives us an accurate picture of what we need to be doing. If we are good listeners, all of our other fathering tasks are likely to improve.

---

1. Who is the best listener you know? What specific things about this person made you list him or her?

---

2. What are the chief distractions that keep us from being the listeners God intended us to be?

---

3. Describe the difference between active listening and passive listening.

4. Where in your home are there no or few interruptions?

5. Think of a time when you were talking to someone and he or she seemed preoccupied. How did it make you feel?

Session Nine: Spiritual Equipping

The Bible urges us to "bring [our children] up in the training and instruction of the Lord" (Eph. 6:4). This covers much more than attending church on Sunday morning.

1. Where are your children learning about God?

2. List ways in which your relationship to your father influenced your perception of God.

3. What is the biggest difficulty you have in attempting to guide your children spiritually?

4. What role do you think worship should play in the task of spiritually equipping your children?

5. What can a father and mother do together to spiritually equip the present generation for future service?

Session Ten: The Eighth Secret

Just as we cannot understand everything about God, we cannot claim to have all of the fathering secrets. In the end, fathering is an experience of mystery and grace.

---

1. Did your father ever extend grace to you? How did he do it?

---

2. In what areas or situations have you encountered the unknowns of fathering?

---

3. In addition to the seven secrets of effective fathers, what secrets would you add?

4. Who has extended a hand of grace to you in the task of fathering? What effect has that act of grace had on your relationship with the person?

5. As you reflect on your feelings for your children, what hopes and fears spring up as you consider the wonder of fathering?

Session Eleven: Review

Reflect on the ideas this book has presented, how they apply to what you knew before, and how you plan on moving forward in your fathering.

1. Of the seven secrets of effective fathers, in which one are you most proficient?

2. Which secret was new or relearned in your thinking about fathering?

3. What secret is missing from your fathering that you would like to add?

4. What other materials or resources have stimulated you as a father?

5. What check-up plans do you have to keep your fathering in good order?

Session Twelve: Fatherlessness: A National Epidemic

Fatherhood, in the sense that I believe God intended it, extends far beyond our own household. Fathering can become a way of outreach, a means by which Christians can affect our society in a powerful, godly way.

1. Identify three children you know who don't have a father.

2. What can you do to reach out to fatherless children?

3. Describe how the current state of fatherlessness has affected our culture, communities, and homes.

4. What can you and your family do to make your home a place of refuge for fatherless children?